Kentucky Bourbon Country

Kentucky Bourbon Country

The Essential Travel Guide

Susan Reigler

Photographs by Pam Spaulding

UNIVERSITY PRESS OF KENTUCKY

Copyright © 2013 by The University Press of Kentucky

Scholarly publisher for the Commonwealth,
serving Bellarmine University, Berea College, Centre
College of Kentucky, Eastern Kentucky University,
The Filson Historical Society, Georgetown College,
Kentucky Historical Society, Kentucky State University,
Morehead State University, Murray State University,
Northern Kentucky University, Transylvania University,
University of Kentucky, University of Louisville,
and Western Kentucky University.
All rights reserved.

Editorial and Sales Offices: The University Press of Kentucky
663 South Limestone Street, Lexington, Kentucky 40508-4008
www.kentuckypress.com

Design by Chris Crochetière, BW&A Books, Inc.
Maps by Dick Gilbreath

17 16 15 14 13   5 4 3 2 1

Cataloging-in-Publication data is available from the Library of Congress.

ISBN: 978-0-8131-4248-7 (hardcover : alk. paper)
ISBN: 978-0-8131-4269-2 (epub)
ISBN: 978-0-8131-4270-8 (pdf)

This book is printed on acid-free paper meeting
the requirements of the American National Standard
for Permanence in Paper for Printed Library Materials.
∞

Printed and bound in South Korea by PACOM KOREA Inc.

Member of the Association of
American University Presses

For Joanna,
who loves bourbon so many different ways

Contents

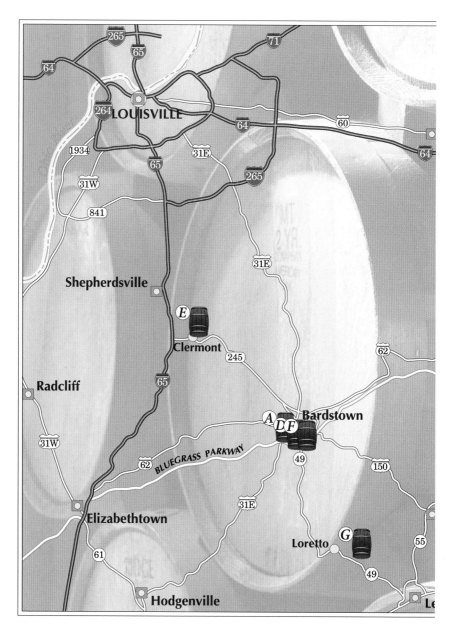

A Barton 1792
300 Barton Road
Bardstown, KY

B Buffalo Trace
1001 Wilkinson Boulevard
Frankfort, KY

C Four Roses
1224 Bonds Mill Road
Lawrenceburg, KY

D Heaven Hill
1311 Gilkey Run Road
Bardstown, KY

E Jim Beam
149 Happy Hollow Road
Clermont, KY

F Kentucky Bourbon Distillers (also
known as Willett Distillery)
1869 Loretto Road
Bardstown, KY

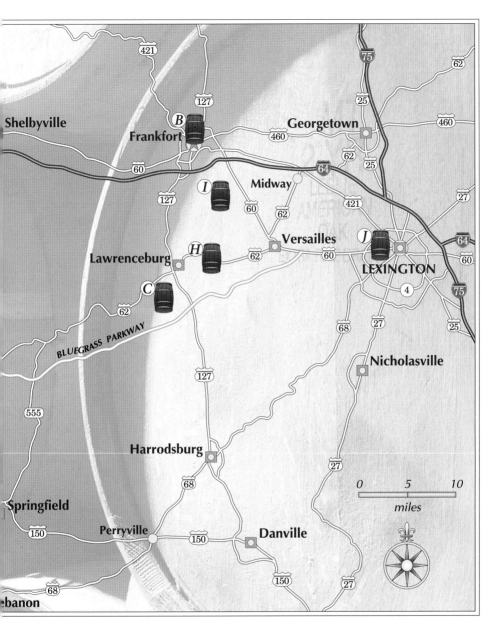

G Maker's Mark
3350 Burks Spring Road
Loretto, KY

H Wild Turkey
1525 Tyrone Road
Lawrenceburg, KY

I Woodford Reserve
7855 McCracken Pike
Versailles, KY

J Town Branch
401 Cross Street
Lexington, KY

Kentucky Bourbon Country

Introduction

Greetings, bourbon-loving traveler, for that is who you are if you have picked up this book. Like a wine lover who dreams of traveling to Bordeaux or a beer enthusiast with visions of visiting the breweries of Belgium, you are probably planning a pilgrimage to Kentucky's bourbon country. This guide will help you get the most out of your bourbon tour of the Bluegrass State.

Between this book's covers you will find information about each of the distilleries that offer tours, as well as other stops of interest to a bourbon aficionado—contemporary and historic sites with bourbon connections, restaurants featuring bourbon-accented dishes, bars with extensive bourbon collections, and even retail outlets that offer a great selection of bourbons, since many brands seldom, if ever, leave the state. Also included are discussions of how bourbon is made and what to look for when tasting and evaluating bourbon, along with a list of bourbon-related terms you will come across in this book and on your distillery tours. Whether you have a long experience of bourbon or are a newcomer to the pleasures of sipping Kentucky's amber elixir, you will find useful information here.

Various aspects of bourbon's history are covered throughout the text, but one striking fact is that before Prohibition was enacted in 1920, more than 200 distilleries operated in Kentucky. After repeal, only 61 reopened. The consolidation of distilleries throughout the twentieth century meant that by 2001, only 10 were operating. Now the numbers are slowly growing again. The existence of nearly 200 different bourbons can be explained by the fact that most distilleries produce several brands.

Bourbon is closely bound to Kentucky's history. It is also important today. According to the Kentucky Distillers' Association (KDA), the bourbon industry directly employs 3,200 people. Taking into account associated industries, such as barrel making and the transportation of ingredients and products, the number of Kentuckians whose jobs are tied to the bourbon industry exceeds 10,000. In fact, during the recession of

2008–2010, the only manufacturers in the state that *added* jobs were the distilleries.

After a decline in bourbon drinking during the second half of the last century, bourbon is now enjoying a global consumer boom. Just over 455,000 barrels were produced in 1999. By 2010, that number had doubled to almost 938,000. Also in 2010, there were 4.7 million barrels of bourbon aging in Kentucky warehouses, surpassing the 4.3 million human population of the state—a statistic that makes a bourbon-sipping Kentuckian feel very secure. According to the KDA, all this distilling activity adds up to some impressive revenues. The distilleries pay some $115 million in local and state taxes, and the industry generates $3 billion in gross state product. Bourbon is obviously a big part of the Kentucky economy.

How to Get to Bourbon Country

Most of Kentucky's bourbon distilleries are found in the central Bluegrass region, within a triangle defined by points at Louisville, Lexington, and Bardstown. If you want to tour on your own, you will need a car, but the drives are easy, and most of the routes are scenic. Much of the eastern portion of this region encompasses Kentucky's famous Thoroughbred horse farms. The area is fairly compact: travel time between Louisville and Lexington and between Lexington and Bardstown is

A typical horse farm in Kentucky.

about an hour, and the drive between Bardstown and Louisville takes about forty-five minutes. So even if you have only one day to devote to touring, it is possible to visit more than one distillery. I would recommend touring no more than two if you also want to try a restaurant where you can enjoy bourbon tastings. If you have at least three days, you can probably visit all the distilleries that offer tours, enjoy several area restaurants, and perhaps visit some of the other attractions listed in this book. If you allow yourself the better part of a week, you will be able to see nearly all the places mentioned here.

The interstate highways serving Kentucky are I-65, I-64, I-71, and I-75. Louisville is a two-hour drive from Indianapolis or Cincinnati, about three hours from Nashville, four hours from St. Louis, five hours from Chicago, and seven hours from Atlanta. The state is also served by three major airports: Louisville International Airport, which most locals still refer to as Standiford Field (http://www.flylouisville.com/); Lexington's Bluegrass Airport (http://www.bluegrassairport.com/); and the Cincinnati/Northern Kentucky International Airport (www .cvgairport.com/).

When to Visit

Spring and fall are probably the best times for a bourbon lover to travel to the state. The weather is mild, with warm days and cool nights, and the countryside is at its prettiest, with either spring blossoms or fall colors. September is National Bourbon Month, and that's when the Kentucky Bourbon Festival is held in Bardstown. Most distilleries suspend operations in July and August, when temperatures soar into the nineties and the humidity climbs. Even though modern fermenters have cooling coils to prevent yeast from dying of excessive heat, cooling can get expensive, so many distilleries use the summertime to perform annual maintenance. Tours are still offered, although you won't see any bourbon being made (but the warehouses, filled with hot barrels of aging and evaporating bourbon, smell fabulous). If you visit in the winter, several distilleries decorate for the holidays and have special evening tours and other events. Just keep in mind that we do get snow and ice in Kentucky, and travel can be tricky.

Whatever time of year you visit, if you are going on distillery tours, be sure to wear comfortable, close-toed shoes. You may have to climb up and down metal stairs, and there may be slippery floors in some facilities.

For information about other (non-bourbon-related) Kentucky attractions, call 800-225-8747 or go to http://www.kentuckytourism.com.

A runner in the Bourbon Chase near Wild Turkey.

KDA Trails

Seven of Kentucky's distilleries—Four Roses, Heaven Hill, Jim Beam, Maker's Mark, Town Branch (part of Alltech Lexington Brewing and Distilling Company), Wild Turkey, and Woodford Reserve—participate in a passport program initiated by the KDA called the Kentucky Bourbon Trail. For more information, go to http://www.kybourbontrail .com. In the fall of 2012, the KDA announced a second travel itinerary: the Kentucky Bourbon Trail Craft Tour is made up of artisanal micro-distilleries, some of which are located outside the area covered by this guide. Included here are the Barrel House Distillery of Lexington and the Limestone Branch Distillery of Lebanon. Visit the Kentucky Bourbon Trail website for current information.

The KDA is also one of the sponsors of an annual 200-mile overnight relay race from Maker's Mark Distillery to downtown Lexington. The course for the Bourbon Chase, held the last weekend in September, goes through several distilleries and a lot of beautiful countryside along the Kentucky Bourbon Trail. For more information, go to http:// www.bourbonchase.com/.

A Word about Kentucky's Other Beverage Industries

As you are traveling through central Kentucky, you will see many signs for wineries. At present, there are more than seventy, and many are open for tours and tastings; several have summer outdoor concert series. If you are interested in visiting a nearby winery, go to http://www.kentuckywine.com/.

There are also several craft beer brewers in the state, mostly in Louisville and Lexington. Information on these brewers, as well as wineries, can be found at http://www.kentuckytourism.com/things_to_do/ wineries_breweries.aspx.

Disclaimer

The information presented in this guide was gathered over three years and is based on my experiences while visiting the distilleries and other attractions. Every effort has been made to provide up-to-date descriptions, but the distilleries do like to add new features. Of course, this makes return visits even more fun. So be aware that there may have been slight changes to the tours described here.

Likewise, I've tried to provide accurate and current listings for restaurants and lodging, but it's always best to call ahead to verify hours and availability.

1. Bourbon Basics

Made in America

To make whiskey, you start by mixing a cooked mash of grain and water; then you add yeast and ferment the mash to produce alcohol. This process actually results in a three-grain beer. If you carry on and distill this liquid to increase its alcohol percentage by volume, you will end up with whiskey. Of course, unless you have a distilling license, this could get you arrested. Although it is legal to be a home brewer or to make wine for your own consumption, the U.S. government does not condone amateur distilling—it would lose too much tax revenue (in Kentucky about sixty cents of every dollar you pay for a bottle of bourbon goes toward state or federal taxes). So when you have a thirst for a drop of whiskey, you'll have to buy it.

As far as can be determined, the first whiskies were made in medieval times, and the place of origin was Ireland or Scotland, depending on which source you credit. The grain used to make Scotch whisky (note: there is no *e* in the spelling) is made primarily of malted barley (that is, the sprouted grains). Rye whiskey uses primarily rye, and bourbon is based on corn. In short, all bourbon is whiskey, but not all whiskies are bourbons.

Bourbon Specifics

Bourbon has some very specific requirements that were codified by Congress on May 4, 1964. By law, bourbon whiskey is "a distinctive product of the United States," so corn-based whiskey can be made anywhere in the world, but it can be called "bourbon" only if it is made in America. The Federal Standards of Identity for Distilled Spirits require the following ingredients and manufacturing techniques for bourbon:

- It must be made of a grain recipe (mash bill) that is at least 51 percent corn.
- It must be distilled to no higher than 160 proof (80 percent alcohol by volume).

Corn, barley, and rye—the grains fermented and distilled for most bourbons.

- It must be aged in new, charred oak barrels.
- Bourbon cannot be put into a container (usually a barrel, but it could be an oak bucket!) at higher than 125 proof (62.5 percent alcohol by volume).
- Bourbon cannot be bottled at lower than 80 proof. Only distilled water can be added to bourbon to adjust the proof.
- No additives of any kind can be used to flavor or color bourbon.
- Bourbon has no age requirement. As soon as the new whiskey touches the oak, it can be called bourbon. Bourbon that has been aged a minimum of two years can be designated "straight bourbon."

- Bourbon aged less than four years must have an age statement on the label.
- If an age is stated on the label, it must be the age of the youngest whiskey in the bottle.

Most bourbon is made with far more than 51 percent corn—usually in the 70s. There is no limit on the amount of corn used: the recipe could be 100 percent corn, and the whiskey would still be bourbon if it met all the other standards. This is different from "corn whiskey," which is aged in used or uncharred cooperage.

There is no requirement regarding the other grains used to make bourbon. Tradition, rather than legislation, has resulted in the use of rye, malted barley, and sometimes wheat. These grains are referred to as the "smalls," since they are used in smaller proportions than corn. In the last few years, some distilleries have produced limited amounts of experimental bourbon using other grains, such as rice.

There is no requirement that bourbon be made in Kentucky, although the vast majority of it, about 95 percent, is. To be labeled "Kentucky bourbon," the whiskey must be distilled in the state and aged in Kentucky for at least two years.

Bourbon Origins

While the definition of bourbon is rigorous, its origin is the subject of speculation and more than a few tall tales. You may even hear some of these tall tales presented as fact on distillery tours. One of the most popular stories is that farmer and Baptist preacher Elijah Craig introduced charred barrels to whiskey making. It seems that his barn caught fire and he didn't want to waste the charred wood, so he made it into barrels to store his whiskey. There is no evidence this is true, but it makes a great story. It may be that when the temperance movement was gathering momentum in the late nineteenth century, claiming that bourbon had been "invented" by a man of the cloth was valuable pro-alcohol propaganda.

What *is* true is that settlers of Irish, Scottish, and German descent brought distilling knowledge (and their stills) with them to the Ohio Valley. Thus, the earliest distillers were farmers, and they dominated whiskey making for several decades. When they arrived, they found that the most abundant grain—the one best suited to the local soil and climate, and the one already being cultivated by the Indians—was corn. Besides being the region's native grain, there was another incentive to grow corn: the "Corn Writs," enacted by Virginia in 1779. As payment for their service in the Revolutionary War, men had been given land in what was then Virginia's westernmost county, Fincastle (Fincastle County would eventually become most of the state of Kentucky). The law stated that anyone who built a cabin and planted a forty-acre patch of corn had a legal claim to the land.

If a farmer's corn crop happened to be significant, storage could become a problem. The grain might rot or be eaten by vermin before it could be used as food, but not if it was distilled. So corn whiskey became both a common beverage on the frontier and a commodity to sell or to use as barter.

Oak trees were abundant in the region, and oak barrels had been used in Europe for centuries to age spirits as well as wine. (By the way, both distillers and wine makers have found that white oak [*Quercus alba*] is the best species for making barrels because it imparts the most desirable flavors.) But why were the barrels charred? Thriftiness (though probably not Elijah Craig's specifically) may be part of the answer. Farmers and merchants used barrels to store many commodities—salt pork, pickles, shellfish—in ice and sawdust. Once these barrels were empty, why not use them to store whiskey? Because most drinkers would shy away from pickle- or oyster-flavored whiskey, the barrels had to be cleaned and any offending odors and flavors erased, which was accomplished by burning off the layer that had come in contact with the previous contents. But would charring *really* exorcise the ghosts of dead fish or pickling brine?

Louisville bourbon historian Michael Veach offers a far more plausible scenario. By the late eighteenth century, one of the major markets for Kentucky's whiskey was New Orleans, a city largely populated by French Loyalists who enjoyed the taste of cognac, a distilled spirit aged in charred oak. (In addition to enhancing flavor and adding color, charring killed microbes that could taint the product.) Brothers Louis and Jean Tarascon fled France during the post-Revolution Reign of Terror and arrived in Pennsylvania in the 1790s. They became interested in the growing trade between settlements in the Ohio Valley and New Orleans and soon started a company in Pittsburgh to ship goods downriver. When one of their vessels was wrecked on the Falls of the Ohio at Louisville, they saw another business opportunity and built a mill and a warehouse on Shippingport Island near the Falls. Cargo-laden boats arriving in Louisville would off-load their goods, store them in a warehouse, and wait for enough rain to raise the water level and make the river navigable. Often they had to wait so long that they lost their customers for nondelivery of the merchandise. These lost sales certainly would have included whiskey, which the Tarascons could buy cheaply, store in charred barrels, and ship south. By the time it arrived in New Orleans months later, the whiskey would have acquired an amber color and some satisfyingly complex flavors. Granted, this story isn't as colorful as the one about the whiskey-making preacher, but culturally, it is certainly plausible.

Finally, there's the question of how bourbon got its name. In 1776 Virginia started dividing Fincastle into smaller counties, including Fayette, where the city of Lexington was located. In 1785 Fayette was divided, and the new county was named Bourbon in honor of the French royal family, in gratitude for France's aid against the British during the War of Independence. At that time, Bourbon County stretched from central Kentucky north to the port of Maysville on the Ohio River. Barrels of whiskey shipped along the Ohio and Mississippi Rivers from Maysville had "Bourbon County" stamped on them to indicate their point of origin, and the whiskey became synonymous with the county. But since we're talking about bourbon, there's another explanation. Remember the cognac-loving French Loyalists of New Orleans, destination of so much of this "red liquor" from Kentucky? Many of their serious drinking establishments were concentrated along a thoroughfare also named in honor of the French royals—Bourbon Street. Was that how bourbon got its name? You are welcome to take your pick of explanations. In any case, by the 1820s the term *bourbon* was being used to specify corn-based whiskey from Kentucky and to differentiate it from rye whiskey produced in Pennsylvania.

How Bourbon Is Made Today

Some of the major developments in the evolution of bourbon making are described in subsequent chapters, but here's an overview of how bourbon is being made in the twenty-first century—a process that has changed little in 150 years. There is some variation from one distillery to the next (a topic covered on the tours), but in general, the first step is to boil milled field corn (not sweet corn) in water to make a hot porridge or mash. A portion of backset (sour mash saved from the previous fermentation) is added to ensure a consistent flavor. When the corn has boiled long enough, the temperature is lowered and rye or wheat, depending on the mash bill, is added. Finally, malted barley is added to the mash. The cooked mash is then pumped into fermenting vats, and yeast and more backset are added. The barley contains enzymes that help convert starches in the grains to sugar, which the yeast then ferments into alcohol.

The water is a very important ingredient and is a key reason why the bourbon industry has flourished in Kentucky. The state's limestone geology means that iron is filtered out of the water as it flows over the rock, and it becomes sweet-tasting mineral water. Whiskey made from water containing iron would turn black, which is absolutely unappealing. All the Kentucky distilleries use either water that comes from springs near or on the distillery property or city water (usually from the Ohio or Kentucky River) that has been filtered to remove fluoride and other chemicals. By the way, limestone's constituent mineral is calcium carbonate, which means that calcium (as well as high amounts of magnesium) is dissolved in the limestone-filtered water. So it is no coincidence that Thoroughbred horse breeding is another signature Kentucky industry. The calcium in the water and in the grass (which absorbs the mineral through its roots) helps build strong bones in the racehorses that drink and graze in the Bluegrass.

Each distillery has its own proprietary strain of yeast. All use brewer's yeast (*Saccharomyces cerevisiae*), but the strains are unique populations of the microorganism. This is important, because the by-products

Mash tub in which grains are cooked.

of fermentation, besides ethyl alcohol and carbon dioxide, are a class of fruity-smelling compounds called esters. Each strain of yeast produces a different ester—some may smell like apples, others like flowers. The complex of esters from a particular yeast strain helps give each bourbon its unique flavor. Change the yeast, and you change the bourbon.

While touring the fermenting room, you will notice vats containing bourbon in various stages of fermentation. At the earliest stage, you will see large, vigorous bubbles. Stick your finger in the vat and get a taste. It will be sweet and taste a lot like hot, corn-flavored cereal. At the final stages, there are only tiny, infrequent bubbles. A taste test will reveal a very tangy flavor, which is why it's called "sour mash."

The result of fermentation is called distiller's beer. Depending on the distillery, the alcohol content at this point is usually between 8 and 11 percent. The distiller's beer is introduced into a column still and pumped to the top. As it trickles down the length of the column, the temperature of the still fluctuates between the boiling point of ethanol (grain alcohol) and the boiling point of water—175 and 212 degrees Fahrenheit, respectively. The alcohol vapor is condensed to produce "low wines," with a concentration of about 55 to 60 percent alcohol by

Fermentation tank where yeast is added to the cooked mash, resulting in distiller's beer.

Column still that turns distiller's beer into low wines.

Thumper No. 1
Cap 15,268.08
P.G. per 24 hours

volume (110 to 120 proof). The low wines are then put into a second still, called the doubler, and redistilled into "high wines" with a greater alcohol content of 65 to 80 percent alcohol by volume (130 to 160 proof).

Some distilleries do not allow the first distillate to condense. Instead, they add what amounts to a low-wine vapor directly into a still called a thumper, which contains hot water. The vapors bubble or "thump" in the water before being condensed as high wines. The clear alcohol is also referred to as "new whiskey" or "white dog" (so named for its high alcohol "bite"). Distilled water is added to adjust the concentration to a maximum of 125 proof before the liquid is put in new charred white oak barrels for aging.

The entire process from milling the grain to producing the new whiskey takes only two or three days. Of course, the whiskey won't be palatable bourbon until it has aged for several years in the oak. Climate also plays a part in bourbon's aging, and Kentucky's hot summers and cold winters are perfectly suited to the process. The barrel wood expands in summer, so the bourbon soaks into the charred portion, called the red layer; then it contracts in winter, forcing the whiskey back into the barrel interior. A few distilleries have climate-controlled warehouses to simulate this temperature cycle, but the vast majority depend on nature.

Because of the evaporation that takes place during aging, the proof when a barrel is "dumped" can be much higher than 125. Again, distilled water is added to adjust the proof. Before bottling, most bourbon is chill-filtered (the temperature is lowered, and the liquid is passed through a paper filter) to remove vegetable solids that could cause cloudiness (referred to as "flocking") when the bourbon gets cold, such as when ice is added. Bourbon can also be filtered using activated charcoal, to which the solid particles stick. Flocking is generally considered undesirable, although a few premium bourbons are sold unfiltered because some bourbon connoisseurs maintain that flocking adds extra flavor. Once bottled, bourbon can last for decades—that is, if you don't drink it first.

The thumper produces high wines, or new whiskey, and increases the percentage of alcohol by volume up to 160 proof.

How to Taste Bourbon

There's nothing mysterious about the art of tasting bourbon, but these tips will help you get the most flavor from your sip—after all, drinking any whiskey is about quality, not quantity. Some bourbons are best enjoyed neat, others with a splash of water; still others lend themselves to mixing in cocktails.

Flavor Profile

Not all bourbon drinkers like all bourbons, which is, of course, one of the reasons there are so many different ones available. Each has a distinctive flavor profile based on half a dozen major factors:

Grain Recipe. The type and pro-portion of grains in the mash bill affect the flavor of the whiskey. Think of how corn bread, whole wheat bread, and rye bread differ in flavor. Now imagine a multi-grain bread baked with different kinds of flour and in a variety of proportions. The mash bill has a similar effect on the flavor of bourbon. By definition, bourbon

Evaluating bourbon in a Glencairn whiskey-tasting glass.

is distilled predominantly from corn and malted barley, and the third grain is usually rye. When wheat is substituted for rye, the resulting whiskey is called a "wheated" bourbon. Again, consider the difference in flavor between rye bread and wheat bread, and you can understand how this factor changes a bourbon's character.

Water. The best water for making any whiskey, including bourbon, is iron free, so the water source is important. Kentucky's limestone-filtered water is excellent for making bourbon. The mineral content gives it a little sweetness and also provides a nutritional boost for the yeast as it carries out the task of fermentation.

Yeast. Yeast does more than turn the sugars in the mash into alcohol. It also delivers a raft of flavors in the form of complex, aromatic molecules called esters, which may have a fruity, flowery, spicy (especially cinnamon), or sweet (especially honey) aroma. If you detect spices in a bourbon's nose, the source is often the yeast, even though many people think rye accounts for this spiciness.

Distillation. The lower the distillation proof, the more concentrated the flavors from the mash bill and the yeast. Whether a column still or a pot still (or both) is used for the distillation can also make a difference, and single, double, and triple distillations have an effect as well. Distilleries make a variety of claims about their distillation processes.

Oak and Aging. The level of char of the oak barrel (from light to dark) and the length of time the bourbon stays in the barrel have a major effect on the bourbon's flavor as well as its color. Aging in oak provides most of bourbon's characteristic vanilla and caramel attributes. Other factors at work in aging include the barrel's location in the warehouse, whether the warehouse is temperature controlled, and the new whiskey's proof when it was introduced to the barrel.

Bottling. Both the proof at which the bourbon is bottled and how it is filtered (chill filtering or active charcoal) can affect the taste. Higher-proof bourbons tend to have greater concentrations of flavor, but they may also be "hotter."

Evaluation

Glassware. The most desirable shape for a bourbon tasting glass is wide at the bottom and narrower at the top. This helps concentrate the vapors from the whiskey as they rise from the liquid. Suitable glasses might be a tulip-shaped wineglass, a brandy snifter, or (perhaps best) a Glencairn whiskey tasting glass (see photo).

Color. Bourbon comes in a range of colors: dark straw, light amber, gold, dark amber, orange, copper, and red. The time spent in the barrel, the depth of the char, and the amount of water added to adjust the proof are all factors in the color.

How to taste bourbon.

Nose. Before you take a taste, put your nose to the top of the glass and, with your mouth slightly open, inhale. The aromas are referred to as the whiskey's "nose," and the action you are performing is called "nosing."

Mouthfeel. When you sip the bourbon, allow it to start at the tip of your tongue and work its way to the back of your throat. The flavor profile will probably change. The sensation in your mouth—the mouthfeel—will range from creamy to oily to light.

Water. After you have tasted the bourbon neat, add a splash (about half a teaspoon) of water to the whiskey. This can release more and different flavors, especially in higher-proof bourbons. It is entirely up to you if you prefer a bourbon with or without water.

Descriptors: Vanilla, Caramel, and More

Everyone's palate is different. For instance, a good friend of mine, whose taste I usually trust implicitly, says that one of my favorite bourbons tastes like "rotting peaches," a flavor I do not detect at all. But this shows the usefulness of having a vocabulary to describe what you taste.

All bourbons have a characteristic vanilla and caramel flavor (more prominent in some than in others), which comes largely from aging in charred oak barrels. Beyond that is a raft of other characteristics that make tasting different bourbons so fascinating. The following list will help you pick out certain aromatics you are smelling or tasting. Not all these elements are present in all bourbons, and they occur in various combinations. Depending on your palate, you will probably detect flavor notes not listed here as well, but these descriptors will certainly give you a start in "speaking bourbon."

Sweetness: brown sugar, burnt sugar, butterscotch, candied fruit, candy corn, caramel corn, honey, maple syrup, marzipan, molasses, spun sugar, toffee

Fruits and Nuts: almond, apple, apricot, banana, black currant, cherry, citrus, dark fruit, date, fig, hazelnut, lemon, nutty, orange, orange peel, peach, pear, plum, red currant, tangerine, walnut

Spices and Flowers: allspice, black pepper, chocolate, cinnamon, clove, clover, cocoa, floral, licorice, mint, nutmeg, peppermint, rose, violet

Other: bacon, butter, cedar, cereal, corn, grainy, grassy, leather, manure, oak, pine, popcorn, smoke, tobacco, wood, wood smoke

2. Louisville

The Beginning of Bourbon Country

When you drive east on Interstate 64 and cross the Ohio River from Indiana into Kentucky, prominent signs along the highway welcome you to "The Birthplace of Abraham Lincoln." You are arriving in Louisville, the state's largest city, with a population of more than 600,000. To the left of the highway is the river's canal, with a series of locks allowing boats and barges to navigate what would otherwise be a stretch of rocky rapids. In 1827 a teenaged Lincoln was one of the laborers who built the original canal.

If you glance into the city to your right as you approach the Ninth Street exit, you'll notice several church spires extending into the sky above a sea of roofs and treetops. These are especially conspicuous at night because they are floodlit. An unexpected skyline structure hovers in the distance that may cause bourbon lovers to think they are having a happy hallucination. It's a giant bottle of Old Forester, which shines like a beacon for incoming whiskey aficionados. Welcome to bourbon country. The sixty-eight-foot-tall bourbon bottle is actually a 100,000-gallon water tank. It sits atop the turn-of-the-century Garneau Building, part of Brown-Forman's corporate headquarters complex on Dixie Highway, just south of Broadway. Beverage giant Brown-Forman makes Old Forester and Early Times at its distillery, located less than three miles south of the

The Louisville skyline.

corporate offices. It also owns Woodford Reserve Distillery and Tennessee whiskey distillery Jack Daniels.

Louisville is a good place to start your exploration of Kentucky's bourbon heritage. The city is a regional transportation hub where three interstate highways converge. Almost all the destinations of interest to a bourbon lover, including the distilleries and the city of Bardstown, are within an hour's drive. (The exception is Maker's Mark Distillery, which is about an hour and a half from downtown Louisville.) With the region's largest selection of hotels and bed-and-breakfasts in a variety of price ranges, Louisville offers accommodations to match any budget.

The city also has a lively and sophisticated restaurant scene. Many kitchens are presided over by nationally recognized chefs who use bourbon in their dishes as routinely as California chefs employ wine. Dozens of these eateries also stock excellent selections of bourbon, and it is not uncommon to be able to order tasting flights (small samples of three or more bourbons). The Louisville Convention and Visitors Bureau has even developed the Urban Bourbon Trail of restaurants and bars, complete with a "passport" and rewards program.

Finally, Louisville's history and economy—from its founding during the Revolutionary War to the present—are intimately bound to the history of bourbon. One-third of the world's bourbon is made there, and visitors will find many sites, past and current, of importance in the development of the bourbon industry.

Louisville

The landmark water tank perched atop Brown-Forman's corporate offices.

What is now Louisville got its start in 1778, when Lieutenant Colonel George Rogers Clark arrived at the Falls of the Ohio with 127 soldiers and about 60 civilian settlers. The party was traveling by boat, and the Falls (actually a series of rapids) was the only nonnavigable portion of the 981-mile-long river, which made it a logical stopping point. They set up camp on an island just off the southern bank of the river, and it became known as Corn Island, for the first crop planted there. (It is highly probable that some of the harvest found its way into a still.) Clark, who was on his way to capture the area north of the Ohio from the British, soon departed with his troops. The direct result of this military campaign is that the United States' northern border with Canada is *not* marked by the Ohio River.

In 1784, the year after the American Revolution ended, a young Welsh immigrant named Evan Williams arrived in Philadelphia and eventually made his way to Louisville. He started a distillery on a site near the riverbank, where the base of South Fifth Street is located today. Williams's

Sidewalk plaque at Seventh and Main Streets showing the location of Corn Island.

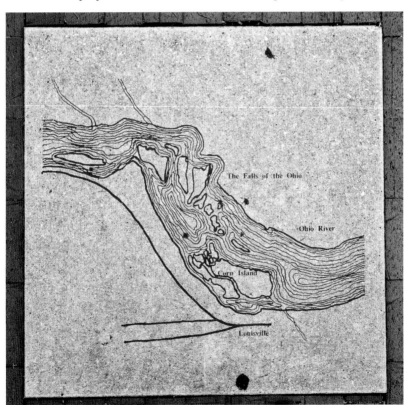

The Pendennis Club.

business has often been cited as the first commercial distillery in Louisville (perhaps in all of Kentucky), but there is no way to verify this claim. Certainly, his distillery was among the earliest and was listed in local tax records in 1789.

By the first decades of the nineteenth century, Louisville had become a center for the whiskey industry. The number of both distillers and rectifiers (merchants who bought bourbon from small-volume distillers and blended it to sell) was increasing steadily. The city's riverside location meant that large quantities of grain could be brought to commercial distilleries by steamboat, which could also transport whiskey throughout the Ohio, Missouri, and Mississippi River Valleys.

This growth peaked after the Civil War, when several blocks of Main Street near the wharf came to be known as Whiskey Row, owing to the large number of distillers and rectifiers headquartered there. Many companies with distilling operations in other parts of Kentucky also had offices on Whiskey Row because Louisville was still the shipping center for bourbon.

In the 1870s two major innovations in the bourbon industry occurred in Louisville. The first came in 1870 when George Garvin Brown, the founder of Brown-Forman, introduced "quality control" by selling his whiskey in sealed bottles. Up until that time, whiskey had been sold from barrels, and it was not uncommon for merchants to dilute the bourbon or mix in additives that could compromise the drink's character. The other innovation is credited to Frederick Stitzel, who operated a distillery with his brother Philip at West Broadway and Twenty-Sixth Street. Concerned that barrels stacked on top of one another put pressure on those below, increasing leaks, and that the lack of air circulation allowed the growth of molds that made the whiskey musty, Stitzel designed a system of racks to hold the barrels in warehouses. He was granted a patent in 1879, and that system is still used throughout the industry today.

Another bourbon-related innovation occurred at Louisville's newly opened Pendennis Club in the 1880s. One of the most prominent members of this private gentlemen's club was bourbon distiller Colonel James E. Pepper, grandson of Elijah Pepper, who in 1812 had built the first distillery on the site of what is now Woodford Reserve. The story goes that another member, a retired Civil War general, did not care for the taste of bourbon (a decidedly unpatriotic attitude in Kentucky), so the club's bartender added sugar, bitters, and water to the general's drink, and the old-fashioned was born. Apparently, the muddled cherry and orange were later modifications.

The original club was housed in a mansion on Walnut Street (now Muhammad Ali Boulevard) between Third and Fourth Streets. The "modern" club was built in 1928, just a block east of the original, at 218 West Muhammad Ali Boulevard. Its bar still serves a lot of old-fashioneds to members.

By the 1890s, the demand for bourbon—whether drunk straight or mixed—was steadily growing both in Louisville and around the country. More and bigger distilleries were built. At the turn of the twentieth century, the massive quantities of corn, rye, and barley required for the bourbon-making boom were transported to the city by rail, and by the end of World War I, more than eighty businesses involved in bourbon making, warehousing, selling, and shipping were located on Main Street. There seemed to be no limit to the potential for growth in the industry. Then, in 1920, came Prohibition.

Although the distilleries closed, Louisville (and Kentucky) still had a large stock of whiskey aging in warehouses. The city almost immediately became America's new "pharmaceutical" hub. The government allowed six companies in the United States to sell "medicinal spirits." Two were in New York City, and the other four—Brown-Forman, Frankfort Distilleries, James Thompson & Bro. (renamed Glenmore Distilling Company in 1926), and A. Ph. Stitzel Distillery—were in Louisville. By 1928, the warehouse supplies were getting low. (Illnesses that required treatment with bourbon seemed to have reached near-epidemic proportions.) Authorities gave the Stitzel distillery permission to make bourbon for the four Louisville distributors.

When Prohibition ended in 1933, a second wave of distillery construction began in Louisville. Seven new distilleries were built southwest of the city before 1940. This area, known as Shively, was outside the incorporated city limits, so the distilleries avoided Louisville taxes. (Eventually, Shively incorporated and enjoyed a tax windfall.)

During World War II, distilleries were required to make industrial alcohol for the military. The war, along with a decline in whiskey drinking that began in the 1960s, resulted in the acquisition of smaller distillers by larger ones and another round of closings. Two large distilleries remain in Louisville today: one operated by Brown-Forman, and the other by Heaven Hill. Neither offers tours, but if you're interested, you can drive by and get a glimpse of the exteriors. It's also possible to drive past the shuttered Stitzel-Weller Distillery, which closed in 1992.

Map Key

1   Asiatique
1767 Bardstown Road

2   The Bar at BLU
280 West Jefferson Street

3   Baxter Station Bar & Grill
1201 Payne Street

4   Bourbon's Bistro
2255 Frankfort Avenue

5   Bristol Bar & Grille Downtown
614 West Main Street #1000

6   The Brown Hotel Lobby Bar
335 West Broadway

7   Buck's Restaurant
425 West Ormsby Avenue

8   Corbett's: An American Place
5050 Norton Healthcare
Boulevard

9   Derby Café at the Kentucky
Derby Museum
704 Central Avenue

10   Dish on Market
434 West Market Street

11   Doc Crow's Southern
Smokehouse & Raw Bar
127 West Main Street

12   Equus & Jack's Lounge
122 Sears Avenue

13   Jockey Silks Bourbon Bar
140 North 4th Street

14   Limestone Restaurant
10001 Forest Green Boulevard

15   Maker's Mark Bourbon House
& Lounge
446 South 4th Street

16   The Old Seelbach Bar
500 South 4th Street

17   Proof on Main
702 West Main Street

18   Ramsi's Café on the World
1293 Bardstown Road

19   The Silver Dollar
1761 Frankfort Avenue

20   The Village Anchor Pub & Roost
11507 Park Road

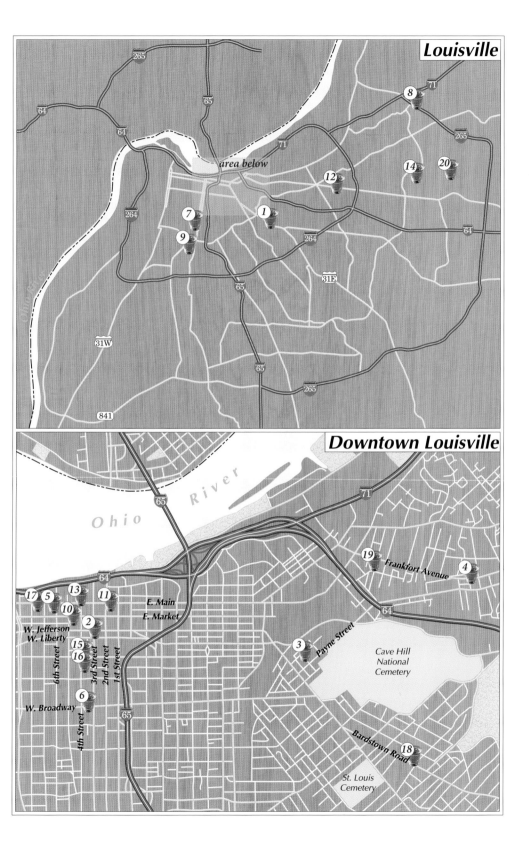

Downtown Louisville and Whiskey Row

Thanks to the renewed popularity of bourbon, combined with community advocacy for historic preservation, Whiskey Row is enjoying a renaissance. Bourbon-related businesses and attractions are returning to the ten-block stretch of Main Street bounded by Brook Street to the east and Ninth Street to the west, and many of these four- and five-story nineteenth-century buildings are being restored and used as offices, condos, restaurants, hotels, and museums. Louisville's Main Street has one of the largest concentrations of cast iron–fronted buildings in the world (second only to New York City's SoHo), making for a very attractive streetscape.

Actors Theatre of Louisville (home of the annual Humana Festival of New American Plays), the Kentucky Center for the Arts (providing concert halls and theaters), Louisville Slugger Field (ballpark for the city's minor league baseball team, the Louisville Bats), and the KFC Yum! Center (a new sports arena and pop music venue) also anchor Main Street. And just as the original Whiskey Row expanded to encompass Market Street, the parallel street one block south of Main, East Market (known as NuLu) has also been revitalized with art galleries, boutique shops, restaurants, hotels, and condos.

One business that endured Prohibition and other changes to Whiskey Row is **Vendome Copper & Brass Works** (www.vendomecopper.com).

Tucked away on a small street just north of the NuLu district, Vendome has been making equipment used to distill bourbon since the early 1900s. The company not only makes equipment for distilleries and breweries throughout the United States but also exports to more than fifteen countries, including to whiskey distilleries in Ireland and cognac distilleries

Detail of a cast-iron facade on Main Street.

Vendome apparatus at the Distilled Spirits Epicenter.

Detail of Vendome distilling equipment at the Distilled Spirits Epicenter.

in France. You could say that Vendome stills are to distilleries what Steinway pianos are to concert halls.

Both Heaven Hill and Brown-Forman have had offices on Main Street for many years, and two new bourbon attractions are scheduled to open on Whiskey Row in 2013 or 2014. **Michter's Distillery** (http://www.michters.com), which traces its roots to eighteenth-century

Pennsylvania, is planning to open the first working distillery on Whiskey Row since before Prohibition. It will be housed in the picturesque 1870s Fort Nelson Building at 801 West Main, topped by an eye-catching turret. Michter's pot stills are being custom made by Vendome. The distillery will offer tours and tastings and will feature exhibits about its whiskey's history, as well as a tasting room and a rooftop garden. The company claims that it made the spirits that warmed Washington's troops at Valley Forge. Master distiller Willie Pratt (formerly of Brown-Forman) will oversee the production of Michter's bourbons at the site. The brand is owned by New York–based Chatham Imports.

Heaven Hill will also have a working microdistillery and bourbon history exhibit at 528 West Main Street. The company's flagship brand, Evan Williams, is named in honor of the historic Louisville distiller, and serendipitously, the **Evan Williams Bourbon Experience** (http://www .evanwilliams.com) will be located just a few hundred yards from what is thought to have been the site of Williams's 1780s distillery. Vendome pot stills will be used to make bourbon here, too. And although this building doesn't have a fancy turret, the four-story-high upturned Evan

Architect's rendering of Michter's Distillery. (Courtesy of Joseph & Joseph)

Evan Williams Bourbon Experience. (Courtesy of Solid Light Inc.)

Williams bottle makes it distinctive. It's actually a fountain that splashes "bourbon" into a very large glass in the lobby of the attraction's exhibition hall.

If you want to learn how to be a distiller yourself, you can take classes eight blocks south of Whiskey Row at the **Distilled Spirits Epicenter** (801 South Eighth Street, 502-301-8130, www.ds-epicenter .com. The center opened in 2012 and houses Moonshine University, the Grease Monkey Distillery, and Challenge Bottling.

Museum Row

Within Whiskey Row is Louisville's modern Museum Row, stretching along West Main Street from Sixth to Ninth Streets. Two stops for sports enthusiasts are the **Muhammad Ali Center** (144 North Sixth Street,

Distilled Spirits Epicenter.

502-584-9254, www.alicenter.org) and the **Louisville Slugger Museum & Factory** (800 West Main Street, 502-588-7228, www.sluggermuseum. org).

Ali is a native of Louisville, and the center named for him features exhibits chronicling the heavyweight boxing champion's career both in the ring and as an advocate for social justice. The exterior of the building, which overlooks the river, is decorated with multicolored tiles that, at a distance, resolve into giant mosaic images of Ali.

The world's largest baseball bat—seven stories tall—leans against the outside of the Slugger Museum. (Note the proportionally large baseball that appears to be lodged in the window of the plate-glass factory next door.) Visitors can watch the famous bats being made and tour interactive exhibits. Everyone leaves with a miniature souvenir bat.

The exhibits of the **Frazier International History Museum** (829 West Main Street, 502-753-5663, http://www.fraziermuseum.org) are centered around the extensive arms collection of founder (and bourbon heir) Owsley Brown Frazier. Everything from a horse-mounted knight in armor to a Remington-toting frontiersman is brought to life. The 10,000-piece toy soldier collection is one of the largest in the United States. The museum also houses the Royal Armouries USA, the only collection of artifacts from the British Royal Armouries (including the Tower of London) on display outside the United Kingdom.

The **Kentucky Science Center** (727 West Main Street, 502-561-6100, http://www.kysciencecenter.org) has interactive exhibits that appeal mostly to children, although visiting exhibits often offer something of interest to adults as well. The IMAX theater in the museum shows films related to science and natural history.

Two museums showcasing regional art and artists are **Louisville Glassworks** (815 West Market Street, 502-992-3270, http://www .louisvilleglassworks.com) and the **Kentucky Museum of Art and Craft** (715 West Main Street, 502-589-0102, http://www.kentuckyarts.org). The former has three working glass studios and offers tours and classes. The latter features exhibits of contemporary Kentucky folk art.

Probably the most unusual museum is the **21C Museum Hotel** (700 West Main Street, 502-217-6300, http://www.21cmuseumhotels.com/ louisville/). The cutting-edge, and often edgy, art is displayed in public exhibition space, on the front sidewalk, and, since this is a hotel, in the bedrooms; it is also integrated into the décor of the restaurant and bar (Proof on Main). Developed by local art collectors Laura Lee Brown (yes, another bourbon Brown) and her husband, Steve Wilson, it is the flagship for a series of museum/hotels they are opening in cities across the country.

Louisville Slugger Museum.

Giant replica of Michelangelo's David *in front of the 21C Museum Hotel.*

Entertainment

Sports, concerts, theater, and other live entertainment can be found downtown between Main Street and Broadway. Call the venues or visit their websites to find out about scheduled events during your visit.

Actors Theatre of Louisville (316 West Main Street, 502-584-1205, http://actorstheatre.org/). This award-wining regional company operates three theaters under one roof. The internationally known Humana Festival of New American Plays is held every March.

The Brown Theatre (315 West Broadway, 502-562-0188, http://www .kentuckycenter.org/AboutUs/BrownTheatre). This historic 1,400-seat venue dates from 1925 and was modeled on New York's Music Box Theatre. Entertainers as diverse as Julie Andrews, David Sedaris, Ladysmith Black Mombazo, and Lyle Lovett have performed here.

Fourth Street Live (South Fourth Street, between West Liberty Street and West Muhammad Ali Boulevard, 502-585-2330, http://www .4thstlive.com). Louisville's modern entertainment district is occupied mostly by chain-restaurant bars and clubs, but two stops on the Urban Bourbon Trail are located here—the **Maker's Mark Bourbon House & Lounge** (446 South Fourth Street, 502-568-9099, www .makerslounge.com) and the **Old Seelbach Bar** in the Seelbach Hilton

Hotel (500 South Fourth Street, 502-585-3200, seelbachhiltonhotel .com).

The Kentucky Center for the Performing Arts (501 West Main Street, 502-562-0100, http://www.kentuckycenter.org). Home to the Louisville Orchestra, Kentucky Opera, and Louisville Ballet, as well as the Broadway Series of touring musicals, the Kentucky Center contains a 2,400-seat main concert hall, a 600-seat theater, and a smaller blackbox theater. Sculptures by Calder, Dubuffet, Nevelson, and Miro are among the artworks permanently installed in the lobby. A half-hour film titled *Kentucky Show!* is screened Tuesday through Sunday and gives a splendid overview of the state's history and culture (http://www.kentuckyshow.com/).

The KFC Yum! Center (West Main Street between Second and Third Streets, 502-690-9000, http://www.kfcyumcenter.com). This 22,000-seat arena opened in 2010 and is the home court of the University of Louisville's men's and women's basketball teams. Among the musicians who have played here are Elton John, the Red Hot Chili Peppers, and Carrie Underwood.

The Louisville Palace (625 South Fourth Street, 502-583-4555, http://www.louisvillepalace.com). This ornately decorated gem of a 1920s movie palace now hosts live concerts as well as a summer film festival of classic Hollywood films.

Louisville Slugger Field (401 East Main Street, 502-212-2287, http://www.batsbaseball.com). A handsome nineteenth-century red-brick train shed was refurbished to serve as the entrance to the stadium home of the Louisville Bats, minor-league affiliate of the Cincinnati Reds. Because of its riverside location, this is a great place to watch the "Thunder over Louisville" fireworks display that kicks off the annual Kentucky Derby Festival.

The Urban Bourbon Trail

In 2009 the Louisville Convention and Visitors Bureau created the Urban Bourbon Trail to promote area restaurants and inform visitors where they could find and drink a variety of bourbons. To be included on the trail, an establishment must have at least fifty different bourbon brands, and a few have more than a hundred. Almost all feature bourbon as an ingredient in their signature dishes. The original trail featured eight places, and as of 2012, that number had grown to twenty.

There are different ways to "travel" the trail, and you get a prize for sipping at several locations. You can pick up a Bourbon Country Passport at the Louisville Visitors Center (301 South Fourth at Jefferson Street, 502-379-6109) or at any of the participating bars and restaurants. This

Bruce and Mary Hemminger of Milwaukee at the Brown Hotel Lobby Bar on the Urban Bourbon Trail.

Brown-Forman master distiller Chris Morris leads a tasting at Bourbons Bistro.

pocket-sized booklet (yes, about the size of a U.S. passport, only thicker) contains descriptions of all the stops along the trail, as well as maps to help you find them and even descriptions and maps of Kentucky's distilleries.

When you visit one of the stops on the Urban Bourbon Trail, have your server or bartender stamp the appropriate page of your passport. When you have made six stops, you can present your passport at the Visitors Center for an Urban Trailblazer T-shirt and a certificate declaring you an official citizen of Bourbon Country. Of course, the real reward is the opportunity to sample a variety of bourbons, including many that seldom make it out of Kentucky, and find some new favorites. There is no time limit, so you do not have to visit all six places in one day.

You can also use the high-tech version of the passport. An Urban Bourbon Trail app is available for both iPhones and Android smart phones. The download is free. Or, if you want a greater challenge than just sampling bourbon at six places, you can download and play SCVGR on the Urban Bourbon Trail, which involves completing assigned tasks or answering questions at each stop. Most of the trail stops are in downtown Louisville, and many are right on Whiskey Row itself. These include Proof on Main, the Bristol Bar & Grille, and Jockey Silks Bourbon Bar at the Galt House Hotel. Other downtown locations are the historic Brown Hotel Lobby Bar, the Old Seelbach Bar, and the Bar at BLU in the Louisville Marriott Downtown.

Even the stops outside the downtown area are not far away and are easy to get to if you have a car. Bourbons Bistro on Frankfort Avenue has more than 130 bourbons and features monthly bourbon dinners (often with master distillers as guests); among its numerous awards, it has been declared an "Icon of World Whisky" by *Whisky Magazine.* Equus & Jack's Lounge in suburban St. Matthews also has frequent dinners and a rotating selection of fine bourbon cocktails, thanks to bar manager Joy Perrine, coauthor of *The Kentucky Bourbon Cocktail Book.*

For more information about the Urban Bourbon Trail and a complete list of participating establishments, visit http://www.bourboncountry. com/urban-bourbon/ or call 888-568-4784.

Churchill Downs and the Kentucky Derby Museum

The Kentucky Derby, first held at Churchill Downs in 1875, is the oldest continuous annual sporting event in the United States. Run on the first Saturday in May, the Derby is often referred to as the Greatest Two Minutes in Sports or the Run for the Roses (referring to the blanket of flowers draped over the winning horse's neck). It tests the stamina and speed of the three-year-old Thoroughbreds racing the Derby's mile and a quarter for the first time in their careers.

Much of what makes the Derby special are its traditions. For what other American sporting event do people actually dress up? Women choose their Derby hats very carefully, and men don equine-themed ties and cufflinks. Just after the bugler in bright red livery plays the "Call to the Post" and the first horse steps onto the track for the parade to the starting gate, the crowd sings the most beautiful of all state songs, "My Old Kentucky Home." The horses that have prevailed here—from Aristides in the very first Derby in 1875 to Gallant Fox, Whirlaway, War Admiral, Citation, Barbaro, and the incomparable Secretariat—represent Thoroughbred racing's elite.

The Greatest Two Minutes in Sports has also spawned what may be the best two weeks of partying in America—the Kentucky Derby Festival. "Thunder over Louisville," a giant fireworks display over the Ohio River in mid-April, signals the start of a series of events that include a hot-air balloon race, a steamboat race, a marathon and mini-marathon for human runners, a parade down Broadway, and countless parties— public and private—where a great deal of bourbon is consumed. During Derby Festival, many master distillers are in town for tastings, bottle signings at liquor stores, and bourbon-themed dinners at local restaurants.

The Derby is such a big deal in Louisville that schools are closed the day before the race and a lot of people take the day off work. Oaks Day (the featured stakes race that Friday is the Kentucky Oaks, for three-year-old fillies) has become Louisville's day at the races, since the Derby itself attracts such a large number of out-of-town visitors.

On Oaks and Derby Days, hawkers move through the grandstand at Churchill Downs selling mint juleps, the signature drink of the Kentucky Derby. Ironically, it isn't made with bourbon. The track uses Early Times Kentucky Whisky, which is aged in *used*, rather than new, charred oak barrels and is therefore not technically a bourbon. (Bourbon lovers are usually relieved to know that no bourbon has been harmed by the addition of minty sugar water and a scoop of crushed ice.)

Whatever the formula, people drink a lot of mint juleps. That Friday and Saturday, more than 120,000 drinks are sold, which requires about 2,000 gallons of Early Times Mint Julep Ready-to-Serve Cocktail (released annually in commemorative bottles by maker Brown-Forman), 1,000 pounds of fresh mint sprigs (for garnish), and 60,000 pounds of crushed ice. And you get to keep the souvenir glass with all the names of previous Derby winners printed on it.

But bourbon can certainly be had, too. Woodford Reserve, the official bourbon of the Kentucky Derby, is used to make $1,000 mint juleps that

Mint julep.

are sold to raise money for horse-related charities. Rare mint varieties and ice from glaciers go into the making of these pricey sips, which are served in polished pewter mint julep cups. For more information about these charity juleps, go to http://www.woodfordreservemintjulep.com.

If you want to attend the Derby or the Oaks, it's a good idea to plan ahead, especially if you want a good seat with an actual view of the horses. The Churchill Downs website has a wealth of information on how to do this (www.churchilldowns.org). Of course, it's much easier to attend races when it's not Derby weekend. Spring and fall meets are held from the last Saturday in April to the end of June and then from the end of October to the end of November.

You can get an excellent feel for the excitement and traditions of the Derby and Churchill Downs any time of year by visiting the **Kentucky Derby Museum** (704 Central Avenue, 502-637-1111, http://www .derbymuseum.org), located near one of the main entrances to Churchill Downs. Interactive exhibits include race simulations, betting, and even the opportunity to mount a life-size model horse in a real starting gate

Statue honoring the late Kentucky Derby winner Barbaro,
at Churchill Downs Kentucky Derby Museum.

(don't worry, there are steps). Other exhibits examine the history and traditions of Churchill Downs and the Derby, and a film shown in an oval, track-shaped theater allows viewers to have the experience of being at the track on Derby Day. You can also take a variety of tours of the track itself, including a historic tour, a tour of the barns and backside, and a behind-the-scenes tour of places the public doesn't usually get to see, including the jockeys' locker room, the press box, and Millionaires Row.

The museum also contains the Derby Café, which serves lunch daily. It is a member of the Urban Bourbon Trail and offers tasting flights (see the museum's website for a list of bourbons available at the café). Of course, you can get an authentic Churchill Downs mint julep there, too.

Churchill Downs and the Derby Museum are about fifteen minutes south of downtown. (The most direct route is along Third Street through historic Old Louisville and past the University of Louisville to Central Avenue.) The museum is open daily except for major holidays.

Locust Grove

Another fifteen-minute drive from downtown, heading east along River Road, will take you to Louisville's most important historic site and the only one in Kentucky that is both a National Historic Landmark and accredited by the American Alliance of Museums. **Locust Grove** (561 Blankenbaker Lane [between River Road and Brownsboro Road (US 42)], 502-897-9845, www.locustgrove.org) was the estate of Colonel William Croghan and his wife, Lucy, who was the sister of Louisville's founder, George Rogers Clark. Croghan served in the American Revolution with George Washington and purchased some land from James and Dolley Madison and Richard and Sarah Taylor (parents of Zachary Taylor).

The graceful Georgian mansion, dating from about 1790, was visited by presidents James Monroe, Andrew Jackson, and Zachary Taylor (who lived on a neighboring estate). Artist and naturalist John James Audubon sketched birds and plants in the surrounding woods for his landmark *Birds of America*. Clark spent the last nine years of his life, from 1809 to 1818, at Locust Grove. His younger brother William, along with his partner Meriwether Lewis, stopped in to see Clark on the way back from their famous expedition to the West.

Tours of the restored mansion and outbuildings introduce visitors to a surprisingly elegant frontier life, but Locust Grove was also a working

View of the mansion and grounds of Locust Grove from Blankenbaker Lane.

farm. The current property consists of 55 of the original 694 acres, providing a period atmosphere that historic sites hemmed in by modern development do not enjoy.

Connections between Locust Grove and bourbon history are twofold. George Rogers Clark was one of the surveyors who laid out Leestown, which is now part of Frankfort and the site of Buffalo Trace Distillery. And one of the farm's products was surely whiskey, since the vast majority of distillers were farmers. The site is so evocative of that history that Heaven Hill used Locust Grove as a location for its orientation film at the Bourbon Heritage Center in Bardstown. (If you have seen the film, you may recognize the little log cabin at the southeast corner of the gardens.)

There may be one more connection to bourbon, or at least to a distiller. In addition to making whiskey, Evan Williams was a brick maker, and his kiln supplied the bricks for many of the early houses in Louisville. All were of approximately the same vintage as Locust Grove, so its bricks might have been made by Williams, too.

The Locust Grove administration is planning to make bourbon a more prominent part of the site's interpretation, so call or visit the website for an update. Meanwhile, Locust Grove is well worth a visit for its history and setting.

The Shively Distilleries Today

Another short drive from downtown, this time west along Broadway to Eighteenth Street, will take you to Louisville's three remaining large distilleries. Two are currently in production, but neither offers public tours.

The administration building at Brown-Forman.

Brown-Forman

If you are driving west on Broadway from downtown, make a left at Eighteenth Street, which becomes Dixie Highway. Two blocks south is a complex of handsome red-brick, ivy-covered buildings resembling a small liberal arts college campus. Only the huge Old Forester bottle looming overhead on your right announces that this is actually the world headquarters of Brown-Forman Corporation (http://www .brown-forman.com).

Brown-Forman actually refers to the complex as the "Campus," which consists of nine office buildings, a bottling plant, and four warehouses. The oldest building dates from 1894, and two are listed on the National Register of Historic Places. Old Forester and Early Times are distilled at the Early Times Distillery (2921 Dixie Highway), about a ten-minute drive south of the Campus. It's no accident that both facilities' settings are notably attractive. The landscaping was designed by Frederick Law Olmsted's firm.

Heaven Hill

Take a left turn onto West Breckenridge, which is just past the white-columned Brown-Forman administration building, and you will arrive at Heaven Hill's Bernheim Distillery. Heaven Hill (http://www.heavenhill.com) makes all its bourbons here, including Evan Williams, Heaven Hill, and Elijah Craig, as well as Bernheim Original Kentucky Straight Wheat Whiskey. The distillery was built in 1991, so it was practically new when Heaven Hill bought it in 1999 from United Distillers, seven years after Heaven Hill's distillery in Bardstown was destroyed by a fire. It contains some of the most state-of-the-art technology in the bourbon industry. The site has seven warehouses, but most of the product made at Bernheim is aged in the company's warehouses south of Bardstown.

Stitzel-Weller

Turn left back onto Dixie Highway, and in a few minutes you'll see the entrance to Brown-Forman's Early Times Distillery on your left. You are now less than a mile from the legendary Stitzel-Weller Distillery.

Founded by Julian P. "Pappy" Van Winkle, it opened on Derby Day 1935. Van Winkle's bourbons were made with wheat instead of rye, were distilled in an all-copper still, and were often aged longer (a decade or more) than standard industry practice. Stitzel-Weller brands included Old Fitzgerald, Very Special Old Fitzgerald 12-Year-Old, Old Weller Antique, and Rebel Yell. Stitzel-Weller was sold in 1972 and was eventually

Warehouses of the Stitzel-Weller Distillery, with the iconic Old Fitzgerald chimney.

acquired by London-based United Distillers (the distilling branch of Guinness PLC). Several brand names were sold to other distillers, which is why they still appear on store shelves, but not necessarily with their original recipes.

What had been United Distillers is now Diageo (http://www.diageo .com), and it still owns the property. Even though all production stopped in the 1990s, several of the company's whiskies are still aged on-site, including those used for the blended whiskey, Crown Royal. Bulleit, the bourbon owned by Diageo, moved its corporate offices to Louisville in 2011. (Diageo also distills I. W. Harper, which is sold only as an export to Asia.) Currently, the Visitors Center is open only to industry salespeople and beverage writers, but there have been rumors that Diageo is considering opening it to the public, so check it out when you are in Louisville.

To get to the site, take Ralph Avenue, the second street on the right, south of Early Times. This leads to Fitzgerald Road, where you will see the rust-streaked, metal-clad warehouses straight in front of you. Turn right onto Fitzgerald, which will take you to the now-gated entrance, but you'll have a good view of the red-brick chimney with "Old Fitzgerald" in white letters.

Where to Eat and Drink

Louisville has a wealth of excellent restaurants, including those that serve southern dishes with a contemporary twist and a plethora of ethnic eateries. There's a growing movement that advocates the use of local and regional ingredients, but since the city is an air hub for shipping giant UPS, restaurants specializing in seafood or any number of international cuisines have access to fresh foodstuffs for their tables, too.

The restaurants participating in the Urban Bourbon Trail reflect this diversity, as do those participating in Louisville Originals (http://www.louisvilleoriginals.com), a consortium of independently owned restaurants that offer a frequent diner rewards program. If you are from another city with an "Originals" program, you can collect and redeem points in Louisville, too. Many restaurants are members of both programs.

The following is by no means a complete list of all the good places to eat in the city. Restaurants have been chosen based on location, consistent quality, and probable appeal to bourbon-oriented visitors, including a good selection of bourbons or bourbon cocktails. Please refer to each restaurant's website for menu details. Participation in the Urban Bourbon Trail and Louisville Originals is designated by UBT and LO, respectively. Pricing is indicated as follows: $—inexpensive, with most entrees priced at $15 or less; $$—moderate, at $16 to $25; and $$$—expensive, at $26 or higher.

Whiskey Row (Main and Market Streets bounded by First and Eighth Streets)

BBC (Bluegrass Brewing Company)—300 West Main Street, 502-562-0007, http://www.bbcbrew.com. Brewpub with Four Roses Bourbon Barrel Loft, $.

Bistro 301—301 West Market Street, 502-584-8337, http://bistro301.com. American, $–$$, LO.

Bristol Bar & Grille Downtown—614 West Main Street, 502-582-1995, http://www.bristolbarandgrille.com. American, $–$$, UBT, LO.

Dish on Market—434 West Market Street, 502-315-0669, http://dishonmarket.com. American, $, UBT.

Doc Crow's Southern Smokehouse & Raw Bar—127 West Main Street, 502-587-1626, http://doccrows.com. Barbeque, $–$$, UBT.

Jeff Ruby's—325 West Main Street, 502-584-0102, http://www.jeffruby.com/louisville.php. Steak house, $$$.

Morton's—626 West Main Street, 502-584-0421, www.mortons.com/louisville. Steak house, $$$.

Patrick O'Shea's Irish Pub—123 West Main Street, 502-708-2488, http://osheaslouisville.net. Has a bourbon cellar, $.

Proof on Main—702 West Main Street, 502- 217-6360, http://www.proofonmain.com/. Contemporary southern/Italian, $$–$$$, UBT.

St. Charles Exchange—113 South Seventh Street, 502-618-1917, http://stcharlesexchange.com. American, $$$. Located in a former distillery.

Vincenzo's—150 South Fifth Street, 502-580-1350, http://www.vincenzositalianrestaurant.com/. Fine Italian dining, $$$, LO.

Z's Oyster Bar & Steakhouse—115 South Fourth Street, 502-855-8000, http://zoysterbar.com/. Seafood and aged steaks, $$$.

Old Louisville

Buck's—425 West Ormsby Avenue, 502-637-5284, http://www.bucksrestaurantandbar.com. Contemporary, $$–$$$, UBT.

610 Magnolia—610 West Magnolia Avenue, 502-636-0783, http://www.610magnolia.com. Contemporary, $$$.

NuLu and Butchertown

Against the Grain—401 East Main Street, 502-515-0174, http://www.atgbrewery.com. Brewpub in Slugger Field, $.

The Blind Pig—1076 East Washington Street, 502-618-0600, http://theblindpiglouisville.com. Gastropub, $$. (The vacant lot next door still contains the foundations of the A. Ph. Stitzel Distillery, which was purchased in 1908 by Pappy Van Winkle and Alex T. Farnsley. Van Winkle's office was in the red-brick building that still stands at the intersection of Story Avenue and Johnson Street.)

Decca—812 East Market Street, 502-749-8128, http://deccarestaurant.com. Contemporary, $$.

Garage Bar—700 East Market Street, 502-749-7100, http://www.garageonmarket.com. Gourmet pizzas, $.

Harvest—624 East Market Street, 502-384-9090, http://www.harvestonmarket.com. Farm to table, $$.

Haymarket Whiskey Bar—331 East Market Street, 502-442-0523, http://haymarketwhiskeybar.com. No food, $.

Rye—900 East Market Street, 502-749-6200, http://ryeonmarket.com. Contemporary, $$$.

Taste Fine Wine & Bourbons—634 East Market Street, 502-409-4644, http://tastefinewinesandbourbons.com. No food, $.

Wiltshire on Market—636 East Market Street, 502-589-5224, http://www.wiltshirepantry/wiltshire-on-market.com. Contemporary, $$.

The bar at the Blind Pig.

Frankfort Avenue/Lower Brownsboro Road

Bourbons Bistro—2255 Frankfort Avenue, 502-894-8838, http://www.bourbonsbistro.com. Contemporary, 150 whiskies, $$, UBT. (Location for monthly meetings of the Bourbon Society, http://www.thebourbonsociety.net.)

Irish Rover—2319 Frankfort Avenue, 502-899-3544, http://www.theirishroverky.com. Pub, $, LO.

North End Café—1722 Frankfort Avenue, 502-896-8770, http://www.northendcafe.com. Contemporary, $–$$, LO.

Pat's Steak House—2437 Brownsboro Road, 502-893-2062, http://www.patssteakhouselouisville.com. Steak house, $$.

The Silver Dollar—1761 Frankfort Avenue, 502-259-9540, http://whiskybythedrink.com. Barbecue, $–$$, UBT.

Highlands

Asiatique—1767 Bardstown Road, 502-451-2749, http://www.asiatiquerestaurant.com. Pacific Rim, $$, UBT, LO.

Baxter Station Bar & Grill—1201 Payne Street, 502-584-1635, http://www.baxterstation.com. Gastropub, $–$$ UBT, LO.

Lunch at Lilly's under a copy of a Howard Christy Chandler mural.

(Warehouses of the former Old Grand-Dad Distillery are located just up the street at the corner of Payne Street and Lexington Road.)

Bistro Le Relais—Bowman Field, 2817 Taylorsville Road, 502-451-9020, http://www.lerelaisrestaurant.com. French, $$, LO.

Jack Fry's—1007 Bardstown Road, 502-452-9244, http://www.jackfrys.com. Contemporary, $$–$$$.

La Bodega Tapas Bar—1606 Bardstown Road, 502-456-4955, http://www.delatorres.com. Spanish, $$, LO.

Lilly's: A Kentucky Bistro—1147 Bardstown Road, 502-451-0447, http://www.lillyslapeche.com. Contemporary southern, $$, LO.

Ramsi's Café on the World—1293 Bardstown Road, 502-451-0700, http://www.ramsicafe.com. International, $–$$, UBT.

Uptown Café—1624 Bardstown Road, 502-458-4212, http://www.uptownlouisville.com. Contemporary, $–$$, LO.

Suburbs

Corbett's: An American Place—5050 Norton Healthcare Boulevard,
502-327-5058, http://www.corbettsrestaurant.com. Contemporary,
$$–$$$, UBT.

Equus & Jack's Lounge—122 Sears Avenue, 502-897-9721,
http://www.equusrestaurant.com. Contemporary, $–$$, UBT, LO.

Limestone—10001 Forest Green Boulevard, 502-426-7477,
http://www.limestonerestaurant.com. Contemporary southern, $$,
UBT, LO.

Majid's—3911 Chenoweth Square, 502-618-2222,
http://www.majidstmatthews.com. Mediterranean, $$.

Village Anchor Pub & Roost—11507 Park Road, 502-708-1850,
http://www.villageanchor.com/. Gastropub, $$, UBT.

Where to Stay

Since tens of thousands of out-of-town visitors descend on Louisville
every year for the Kentucky Derby, the city usually has no shortage of
hotel rooms. Virtually all the national hotel and motel chains have a
presence here, many with multiple locations, and there is a wide price
range.

One way for bourbon-oriented visitors to have a true local experience
is to stay at one of the major downtown hotels, including two venerable

Dining room at the 1840 Tucker House Bed-and-Breakfast.

establishments dating from the early twentieth century—the Brown Hotel and the Seelbach Hilton Hotel. Another great way to experience the city is to stay at one of several locally owned bed-and-breakfasts, many of which are located in the Victorian Old Louisville neighborhood south of the city center and north of Churchill Downs. They cost less than downtown accommodations but a little more than budget hotel chains. Bear in mind that you get a delicious and filling breakfast included in the tariff.

Rates listed here are the establishment's lowest. Special features and suites cost more, and daily rates can vary, so you will probably be quoted a higher rate, depending on when you want to stay.

Downtown Hotels

The Brown Hotel—335 West Broadway, 502-583-1234 or 888-387-0498, http://www.brownhotel.com. $189. The Brown's Lobby Bar is on the Urban Bourbon Trail.

Galt House Hotel—140 North Fourth Street, 502-589-5200 or 800-843-4258, www.galthouse.com. $135. The Galt's Jockey Silks Bourbon Bar is on the Urban Bourbon Trail.

Hyatt Regency—320 West Jefferson Street, 502-581-1234 or 800-633-7313, louisville.hyatt.com. $143.

Louisville Marriott Downtown—280 West Jefferson Street, 502-627-5045 or 800-533-0127, www.marriottlouisville.com/. $219. The Bar at BLU is on the Urban Bourbon Trail.

Seelbach Hilton Hotel—500 South Fourth Street, 502-585-3200 or 800-333-3399, www.seelbachhilton.com. $165. The Old Seelbach Bar is on the Urban Bourbon Trail.

21C Museum Hotel—700 West Main Street, 502-217-6300 or 877-217-6400, http://www.21cmuseumhotels.com/louisville/. $229. Proof on Main is on the Urban Bourbon Trail.

Bed-and-Breakfasts

The Louisville Bed-and-Breakfast Association has nineteen member inns. Rates average $100 to $120 per night for a room and breakfast for two adults. For a list of all the B&Bs, with links and phone numbers, go to http://www.louisvillebedandbreakfast.org.

Mint Julep Tours

This Louisville-based tour company has a fleet of comfortable passenger vans and offers a variety of Louisville and Kentucky experiences. Mint

Mint Julep Tours.

Julep can provide a designated driver for your Urban Bourbon Trail crawl, take you around the city for a tour of historic places or a shopping spree, or offer guided day visits to nearby horse farms or distilleries. If you are interested in visiting the Brown-Forman Cooperage, you will have to book the tour through Mint Julep. Mint Julep can even arrange for you to select your own barrel of bourbon at a distillery. This will set you back a few thousand dollars, but you won't have to buy bourbon again for a very long time.

For details about all the tours, go to www.mintjuleptours.com. For pricing information, call 502-583-1433. Tours leave from the Galt House Hotel, where the company has an office and a gift shop on the third floor, Suite 326, in the Retail Row of the Rivue Tower.

Bourbon Balls and Beyond

Many of the distillery tours offer bourbon balls made with the distillery's whiskey, in addition to drink samples. Most of these candies are produced by either Rebecca Ruth of Frankfort (http://www.rebeccaruth.com) or Ruth Hunt Candies of Mt. Sterling (http://www.ruthhuntcandy.com). Several candy makers in Louisville also make bourbon balls, including Muth's, which has been in business since 1921, and Cellar Door Chocolates, established in 2007 (and the subject of a feature story on NPR's *Morning Edition*). Located in the Butchertown Market, Cellar Door makes an impressive assortment of sixteen different bourbon balls, from basic dark chocolate to those laced with mint, ginger, honey, caramel, and even cayenne. Owner and chocolate maker Erika Chavez-Graziano uses some ingredients from her neighbor, Bourbon Barrel Foods, including bourbon-smoked sugar for her cotton candy and bourbon vanilla sorghum in one of her specialty truffles.

Bourbon Barrel Foods also got its start in 2007 and received some good press in several media outlets, including the *New York Times*. Proprietor Matt Jamie ages his micro-distilled soy sauce, Worchestershire sauce, and vanilla extract in used bourbon barrels. He also smokes paprika, coarsely ground sea salt, and black pepper using bourbon. The flavors are intense and wonderful. The vinaigrette salad dressing made with sorghum and Woodford Reserve bourbon is addictive.

In the gift shops at Jim Beam,

A selection of gourmet foodstuffs from Bourbon Barrel Foods of Louisville.

Wild Turkey, Buffalo Trace, Maker's Mark, Woodford Reserve, and Heaven Hill, you will find an array of foodstuffs made with each company's brands, including steak sauces and marinades, barbecue sauces, and hot sauces. Jim Beam also has a very good chicken-wing sauce, and Wild Turkey sells bourbon-smoked jerky in its shop. On the sweet side, try the bourbon cherry preserves from Buffalo Trace, as well as its fudge and caramel sauces. Most of the distilleries have bourbon-accented pancake syrups, too. And you can turbo-charge your Manhattan or old-fashioned with maraschino cherries soaked in Maker's Mark.

Many of the large liquor stores listed in appendix B carry several brands of bourbon food products, such as bourbon-coated nuts of different varieties. You may even encounter bread and pancake mixes made with spent mash.

In the past decade, several craft breweries have started using bourbon barrels to age specialty beers to impart extra flavor. If you can get it, Allagash of Maine makes a remarkable Curieux Bourbon Barrel Aged Triple Ale. Among other national craft brewers that produce a bourbon ale or stout are Goose Island of Chicago and Full Sail of Oregon. When you are in Kentucky, look for Bluegrass Brewing Company's Bourbon Barrel Stout and All-Tech Brewing's Kentucky Bourbon Barrel Ale.

If you want to try your hand at making dishes with bourbon, get a copy of *The Kentucky Bourbon Cookbook* by Albert Schmid (2010, University Press of Kentucky, $24.95) or *Splash of Bourbon: Kentucky's Spirit: A Cookbook* by David Domine (2010, McClanahan Publishing House, $29.95).

The following establishments in Louisville sell bourbon candies and other foodstuffs:

Art Eatables Small Batch Bourbon Truffles—502-751-1208, http://www.arteatables.com/

Bluegrass Brewing Company (main location)—3929 Shelbyville Road, 502-899-7070, http://www.bbcbrew.com/

Butchertown Market—1201 Story Avenue—where the following are located:

> Bourbon Barrel Foods—502-333-6103, http://www.bourbonbarrelfoods.com
> Cellar Door Chocolates—502-561-2940, http://www.cellardoorchocolates.com

Dundee Candy Shop—2212 Bardstown Road, 502-452-9266, http://www.dundeecandy.com/

Ghyslain on Market—721 East Market Street, 502-690-8645, http://www.ghyslain.com

Muth's Candies—630 East Market Street, 800-556-8847, http://www.muthscandy.com

And just across the river from downtown Louisville is Schimpff's Confectionary—347 Spring Street, Jeffersonville, Indiana; 812-283-8367, http://www.schimpffs.com/.

3. Frankfort and Midway
Buffalo Trace and Woodford Reserve

When Kentucky became a state in 1792, officials in both Louisville and Lexington believed their respective cities should become the capital. The new state legislature decided to take bids, and the city offering the best deal would win the honor. A Frankfort landowner agreed to provide property for government buildings, the materials to construct them, a percentage of rents from his tobacco warehouses, and the princely sum of $3,000. So tiny Frankfort (current population 27,000, compared with Louisville's 600,000 and Lexington's 300,000) became the seat of the state government.

Thanks to its location on a double bend in the limestone-rich Kentucky River, Frankfort was also a suitable location for distilleries. Before 1920, more than a dozen operated in the city and surrounding Franklin County, including the Frankfort Distillery Company, which was allowed to bottle stored whiskey for "medicinal" purposes during Prohibition. Many of the brands produced in Frankfort are still made today, though not necessarily in Frankfort. They include Old Fitzgerald, Four Roses, and Ancient Age. Other colorful brand names are now only a memory, such as Kentucky Triumph, Golden Phantom, and Old Woodpecker. Frankfort was also home to the unfortunately named Swastika bourbon. Today, Buffalo Trace is the capital's only operating distillery. Jim Beam has a bottling operation in Frankfort (3200 Georgetown Road), but it is not open for tours.

Other than Buffalo Trace, the Frankfort attraction of most interest to bourbon lovers is the **Rebecca Ruth Candy Tours and Retail Store** (112 East Second Street, 800-444-3766, http://www.rebeccaruth.com). Founders Ruth Hanly Booe and Rebecca Gooch started their candy-making business in 1919. They are credited with inventing that staple of Kentucky confections, the bourbon ball. The classic bourbon ball is a dark chocolate bonbon laced with bourbon (the Rebecca Ruth brand uses Evan Williams) and topped with a roasted pecan. The store is open Monday through Saturday from 9 a.m. to 5:30 p.m. Tours that let you watch the candy being made are offered daily from 9 a.m. to noon

Kentucky's Beaux-Arts state capitol

Rebecca Ruth candy factory and shop.

and 1 to 4:30 p.m., except during the store's busy seasons: Christmas, Valentine's Day, Mother's Day, and Easter. There is a small charge for the tour.

Your best destination for sampling bourbon in Frankfort is **Serafini Restaurant & Bar** (243 West Broadway), which stocks a large selection of bourbons and hosts frequent tastings and bourbon dinners. On the same block are Poor Richard's Books (a splendid independent bookstore), the Kentucky Coffee Tree Café (a great place for lunch), and Capital Cellars Wine & Spirits Café (an excellent place to buy bottled bourbons).

To see the style in which some bourbon magnates lived pre-Prohibition, visit the **Berry Mansion** (700 Louisville Road, 502-564-3000, http://www.historicproperties.ky.gov/hp/berrymansion/). The twenty-two-room colonial revival–style mansion was built on a bluff overlooking the capitol by George and Mary Berry in 1900. Berry was the chief executive of the Old Crow Distillery, the ruins of which are still standing in Millville (see pages 85–87).

If you have an interest in Kentucky history, the **Thomas D. Clark**

Center for Kentucky History (100 West Broadway, 502-564-1792, http://www.history.ky.gov) is worth a visit, as is the beautiful 1910 Beaux-Arts **State Capitol Building** (700 Capital Avenue, 502-564-3449, http://wwwhistoricproperties.ky.gov).

A free trolley stops at various attractions all around the city. You can find a trolley schedule, as well as more information about Frankfort attractions, at http://www.visitfrankfort.com. The city's Visitors Center is located in a pretty Victorian house at 100 Capital Avenue, near the Rebecca Ruth store. You can stop in there for maps and other advice on touring the city, or call 800-960-7200.

Where to Eat and Drink

You'll find a lot of chain outlets along US 127 and US 60 leading into Frankfort. The eateries listed here are independently and locally owned. Pricing is indicated as follows: $—inexpensive, with most entrees priced at $15 or less; $$—moderate, at $16 to $25; and $$$—expensive, at $26 or higher.

Adelia's Bakery & Café—1140 US 127 S, 502-227-9492, http://www.links2thebluegrass.com/Adelias.html. $.

Bistro 241—241 West Main Street, 502-352-2412. $$.

Capital Cellars Wine & Spirits Café—227 West Broadway, 502-352-2600, http://capitalcellars.net/. $.

Kentucky Coffee Tree Café—235 Broadway, 502-875-3009, http://www.kentuckycoffeetree.com/. $.

Rick's White Light Diner—114 Bridge Street, 502-330-4262, http://rickswhitelightdiner.com/. $.

Serafini Restaurant & Bar—243 Broadway, 502-875-5599, http://www.serafinifrankfort.com/. $–$$$.

Historic 200 block of West Broadway.

Where to Stay

Many of the national hotel and motel chains, including Days Inn, Best Western, and Hampton Inn, have outlets in Frankfort, located along the US 127 and US 60 corridors. Other options include the following:

The Capital Plaza Hotel—405 Wilkinson Boulevard, 502-227-5100, http://www.capitalplazafrankfort.com. The Terrace restaurant has a good bourbon selection.

Meek House Bed & Breakfast—119 East Third Street, 502-227-2566, http://www.bbonline.com/united-states/kentucky/frankfort/meek .html.

The Meetinghouse Bed & Breakfast—519 Ann Street, 502-226-3226, http://www.themeetinghousebandb.com/.

Buffalo Trace Distillery

1001 Wilkinson Boulevard
Frankfort, KY 40601
502-696-5926
http://www.buffalotrace.com

Hours: Monday–Friday, 9 a.m.–5 p.m.; Saturday, 10 a.m.–5 p.m.; Sunday, noon–5 p.m. Tours are available year-round and start on the hour. The last tours start at 3 p.m. Closed on major holidays. Call for information about special tours offered at other times.

Bourbons: Ancient Age, Ancient Ancient Age, AAA 10 Star, Benchmark, Blanton's Single Barrel, Buffalo Trace, Eagle Rare 17-Year-Old, Eagle Rare Single Barrel, Elmer T. Lee, George T. Stagg, Hancock's President's Reserve, Old Charter 101, Old Charter 8-Year-Old, Old Charter 10-Year Old, Old Rip Van Winkle 10-Year-Old (90 and 107 proof), Old Taylor, Old Weller Antique, Pappy Van Winkle's Family Reserve 15-Year-Old, Pappy Van Winkle's Family Reserve 20-Year-Old, Pappy Van Winkle's Family Reserve 23-Year-Old, Rock Hill Farms, Van Winkle Special Reserve 12-Year-Old, William Larue Weller, W. L. Weller 12-Year-Old, W. L. Weller Special Reserve

Ryes: Sazerac Rye 18-Year-Old, Sazerac Straight Rye Whiskey, Thomas H. Handy Sazerac, Van Winkle Family Reserve Rye

Other Liquors: Buffalo Cream Liqueur (made with bourbon), Buffalo Trace White Dog (not aged), Rain Vodka (made with organic white corn)

Chief Executive: Mark Brown
Master Distiller: Harlen Wheatley

Buffalo Trace Distillery.

Master Distiller Emeritus: Elmer T. Lee
Owner/Parent Company: Sazerac Company
Tours: Several different tours examine different aspects of the distillery, so repeat visits are worthwhile. Visitors are given a choice of bourbons to taste at the tour's conclusion.
What's Special:
- Situated on 130 acres on the banks of the Kentucky River, Buffalo Trace contains more than 100 buildings whose construction spans four centuries.
- Whiskey was first distilled on this site in 1787.
- This was one of only four distilleries allowed to operate during Prohibition to make "medicinal" whiskey.
- Buffalo Trace contains the world's smallest aging warehouse, which accommodates a single barrel.
- It maintains an experimental program producing very limited, special-edition whiskies.
- In December, holiday light displays decorate the grounds, which visitors can tour by car after sunset.
- The distillery was featured in a November 2011 episode of *Ghost Hunters* (SyFy), and an evening Ghost Tour was developed as a result.
- Rain is the only U.S.-made vodka for which the entire process, from grain to bottle, occurs at one distillery.
- Company offices are housed in Stony Point Mansion (completed in 1934) on Rock Hill, overlooking the distillery.

Distillery tour.

- Landscaped gardens and a log clubhouse dating from 1935 can be rented for events.
- The Independent Stave Cooperage Museum is located on-site.

History

The green, rolling landscape of Kentucky's Bluegrass region, populated by grazing Thoroughbreds, is iconic, seemingly timeless. But the horses and the bluegrass pastures are newcomers. For thousands of years before the arrival of white settlers, the land was covered in forests and tracts of tall native cane, and herds of American bison (or buffalo) dominated the landscape. These herds trampled wide paths through the plant cover, crossing rivers at points where the water was shallow enough for the animals to ford. Many eighteenth-century pioneers used these paths, called buffalo traces, to gain access to the wilderness interior.

Buffalo Trace Distillery is located on the eastern bank of the Kentucky River near Frankfort, where buffalo once crossed the waterway. Whiskey has been made on the site for more than 200 years. Ironically, the current name dates only from 1999, so it is even more recent than the horses and the bluegrass.

In 1775 brothers Hancock and Willis Lee of the Ohio Company, assisted by a twenty-two-year-old surveyor named George Rogers Clark (future Revolutionary War hero and founder of Louisville; see "Locust Grove" on page 47), established the settlement of Leestown "on the Buffalo Trace." Hancock Lee started distilling, which was a common practice on the frontier. As Henry Crowgey notes in *Kentucky Bourbon: The Early Years of Whiskeymaking*: "People moved in [to Kentucky] who regarded liquor as a necessity of life. The distillation of liquor or brandy occupied the same place in their lives as did the making of soap, the grinding of grain in a rude handmill, or the tanning of animal pelts; distilling equipment was as necessary as the grain cradle, the hand loom, or the candle mold."

The ready supply of limestone water and corn for the whiskey and oak for the barrels meant that distilling continued to flourish at the riverside location just downstream from Kentucky's new state capital. It also didn't hurt that the barrels could be loaded onto boats docked right beside the distillery. The whiskey, distilled by one Harrison Blanton starting in 1812, was shipped down the Kentucky, Ohio, and Mississippi Rivers to New Orleans, where there was considerable demand for it.

Distilling continued at Leestown through the Civil War. In 1870 Edmund Haynes Taylor Jr. (great-nephew of President Zachary Taylor)

Barrels being loaded at Buffalo Trace.

bought the property and began the process of modernizing and industrializing the whiskey-making process. He named his operation "O.F.C." (Old-Fashioned Copper) because he was using an all-copper distilling apparatus. Taylor's other innovation was to introduce steam heat to the warehouses. The distillery changed hands again when George T. Stagg bought it in 1878. And in 1897 teenager Albert B. Blanton joined the company as an office boy. Eventually, he would become superintendent of the distillery's operations and finally president of the George T. Stagg Distillery.

It was Blanton who steered the distillery through the dismal years of Prohibition, when it was one of only a few facilities in the country licensed by the federal government to make liquor for "medicinal" purposes. This was prescient on the part of the feds, since a remarkable round of ailments afflicted Americans between 1919 and 1933. For example, the distillery bottled 1 million pints of medicinal bourbon in 1925, and some 6 million prescriptions for bourbon were written in Kentucky alone before the repeal of Prohibition.

The distillery went through a couple of name changes, becoming Blanton's and then Ancient Age, in honor of its flagship brand. Colonel Blanton (as he came to be known) retired in 1952, the same year that Warehouse V was built. The small building stores a single aging barrel, and in 1952, it housed the two millionth barrel produced at the facility since Prohibition's end. The current resident is the six millionth barrel. When it's ready to drink, the bourbon from the barrel in Warehouse V is bottled in special commemorative packaging and donated to selected charities to be auctioned off for fund-raising.

The barrel-run crossing, with tiny Warehouse V in the background.

Corn being dispensed by a delivery truck at Buffalo Trace.

In 1968 Elmer T. Lee became distillery manager. Lee can claim the distinction of introducing the first single-barrel bourbon, Blanton's, named in honor of his predecessor. (You have probably noticed that the names of many of the bourbons made at Buffalo Trace today are associated with the distillery's very long history.) Lee retired the following year; he is now in his nineties and remains master distiller emeritus.

In 1992 Ancient Age Distillery was purchased by the Sazerac Company, a family-owned business based in New Orleans. After some remodeling and updating, the distillery reopened as Buffalo Trace in 1999, the same year its new eponymous flagship brand was introduced.

The Tours

Given the size and history of Buffalo Trace, it is not surprising that no single tour provides the complete story of the place. But it is possible to do as many as three tours in a single day, if you're willing to devote yourself to this one site. Alternatively, you can schedule repeat visits.

All the tours are free, although some require advance reservations. They all end with a free tasting. There's even root beer for those who are under twenty-one or abstemious. (It may be hard to imagine, but some people are just interested in the history, rather than the beverage itself.) If you do indulge, try Buffalo Trace's version of a grown-up root beer float. I won't give away the secret ingredient here.

Check in at the Visitors Center for all the tours. While waiting for your tour to start, you can peruse the collection of bourbon history memorabilia, which includes one of those 6 million Prohibition-era prescriptions, and browse the gift shop. Tip: Try the Buffalo Trace cherry preserves laced with bourbon. They aren't just for your breakfast toast. Try them over vanilla or chocolate ice cream.

The Trace Tour

This is a walk-in tour, with no reservations required. It occurs daily on the hour and lasts for about an hour. A fifteen-minute orientation film covers bourbon's history and ingredients, especially in relation to the Leestown location. Not until the lights go up and your guide opens a disguised door (I won't reveal this secret, either) into a warehouse do you realize your close proximity to the film's subject.

If you visit during the workweek, you'll be able to see the bottling operation in action. The insider's information imparted by your guide may include details about the little horse figurines atop the stoppers on bottles of Blanton's Single Barrel Bourbon. Warehouse V, the world's smallest whiskey-aging structure, is another tour highlight.

The distillery grounds are beautifully landscaped, and if the day is fine, you might enjoy a stroll around them. Don't miss the fascinating trompe l'oeil mural painted on a wall across from the gardens and log clubhouse. The perspective shifts as you walk past the painting.

Visitors on a tour walk past a trompe l'oeil mural of a warehouse.

The Post-Prohibition Tour

After Prohibition ended, the demand for now-legal spirits skyrocketed, and the distillery experienced a building boom. On this tour, guides focus on the distillery's architecture and modernization from 1930 to 1950. Much of the tour centers around Colonel Blanton's contributions, including the two-story log clubhouse he had built from disassembled 100-year-old log cabins and the stone mansion that was his home. You'll also see the distillery's only metal-clad warehouse (Warehouse H, with a capacity of 15,000 barrels) and the enormous Warehouse I, which stores an impressive 51,000 barrels. Reservations must be made in advance, since this tour is given only when there is demand.

The Hard-Hat Tour

This reservation-only tour is available only when the distillery is operating. If you are interested in the minutiae of bourbon making, you'll love it. Be prepared to climb up and down a lot of metal stairs and along an enclosed catwalk. If the timing is right, there may be a corn delivery, and you can watch the grain being emptied from the truck. The entire process—from the mash cookers (giant pressure cookers) to the fermentation tanks to the column stills (three stories high)—is on display. Perhaps most interesting is the room where yeast colonies were stored when the distillery kept them on-site. The tanks are still there, as well as gleaming antique distillation equipment and historic photos of the distillery.

The tour wraps up by the riverbank, where plaques on the corner of a building mark the water levels from historic floods. You do not actually have to wear a hard hat, but open-toed shoes are not allowed.

The Ghost Tour

Again, reservations are required for this tour, which is offered Thursday through Saturday evenings at 7 p.m. and 9 p.m. Even if you are a die-hard skeptic, it is terrific fun. From October to March, it takes place after dark, which creates a whole different atmosphere. Paranormal investigators from Lexington have identified at least twenty-seven different spirits (be prepared for almost endless puns on this word), including Colonel Blanton himself. Visitors climb aboard a van that goes to the mansion where he died (the guide will point out the actual room). It's appropriately creepy that the colonel had a spider-web design etched into the glass of the front door.

The SyFy television network's *Ghost Hunters* filmed a program here and declared it a very haunted site. The good news is that, by all accounts, Buffalo Trace's ghosts are a pretty jolly band of spooks

Visitors photograph some elusive spirits on the Ghost Tour.

who have lingered because they love the place so much. (What bourbon lover wouldn't want to spend eternity in a distillery?) The tour guide will point out places where there have been "sightings," including the upper-story window in the abandoned eighteenth-century house near the river, where someone allegedly saw a hand drawing back a curtain from a long-curtainless window in a room that has no floor.

You might not spot any ghosts on the tour, but you could feel the hairs rising on the back of your neck when the lights are turned out in Warehouse C. In the pitch dark, you realize that several thousand tons of sleeping bourbon are perched over your head. It's very much like the moment in a cave tour when the guide kills the lights, except that the evaporating bourbon makes the warehouse smell oh-so-much better.

If you want to take in multiple tours in one day, keep in mind that the Hard-Hat Tour is offered in the morning. You could go on that one, have lunch at the distillery's Firehouse Café, and then take the Trace Tour in the afternoon. Thursday through Saturday, you could also take an afternoon tour, go into Frankfort for dinner, and return for a Ghost Tour.

The **Firehouse Café** (502-783-5673, firehousecafe@ymail.com) is located behind Warehouse C and is open from May to October. Lunch is served Tuesday through Saturday. The building formerly housed the distillery's working fire department and contains a display of equipment, including a bright-red vintage 1964 Ford fire truck. You can order box lunches for parties of ten or more by calling or e-mailing at least twenty-four hours in advance.

The Bourbon

Spirits made at Buffalo Trace have earned more than 200 industry awards, outperforming all other distilleries. Of course, it makes more different brands of bourbon (plus rye and corn-based vodka) than any other distillery, so it has something of a head start. End-of-tour tastings offer only a fraction of its products, but bourbon lovers will not be disappointed. You can sample any two of the following: Buffalo Trace, Eagle Rare, Rain Vodka, White Dog, and Buffalo Trace Bourbon Cream. Kentucky law allows a maximum of two small samples per person per tasting, so choose carefully.

Master distiller Harlen Wheatley and master distiller emeritus Elmer T. Lee know their craft and are making some very elegant beverages, so any Buffalo Trace brands you come across in stores around the country will be worth trying. Julian Van Winkle III also retains a hand in production, overseeing the distillation, aging, and bottling of the premium

Van Winkle bourbons made at Buffalo Trace, based on those his family formulated at the now-closed Stitzel-Weller Distillery in Louisville.

Providing complete tasting notes for all the bourbons made here is beyond the scope of this book, and since the distillery is privately held, it does not release information about the exact percentages of the grains used in its mash bills. That said, certain

Guide Fred Mozenter offers tastings at tour's end.

characteristics noted here can help you understand the different flavor profiles.

Buffalo Trace uses two mash bills (grain percentages) in its bourbons made with corn, rye, and malted barley. Other factors, such as aging, mingling, and proof, provide the distinctive flavor profiles of each brand. Mash bill 1 is used for Buffalo Trace, Eagle Rare, Old Charter, and George T. Stagg. Mash bill 2 contains a higher percentage of rye and is used to make Blanton's, Elmer T. Lee, and Rock Hill Farm bourbons.

Among the wheated bourbons made here (wheat is substituted for rye in the mash bill) are all the bourbons with "Weller" or "Van Winkle" in their names, including W. L. Weller, William Larue Weller, Old Rip Van Winkle, and Pappy Van Winkle.

Although the two bourbons available at the tour tastings—Buffalo Trace and Eagle Rare—are both made with the same mash bill and bottled at 90 proof, you will taste a difference. Buffalo Trace is a small-batch bourbon, which in this case means that anywhere from 100 to 125 barrels are chosen for a bottling's mingling, and it is aged between eight and nine years. Eagle Rare is bottled from a single barrel and is aged for ten years (another expression is aged seventeen years). Both exhibit a cinnamon-spicy nose and plenty of caramel and fruit, but you may find a little more sweetness in the middle of the Buffalo Trace, with more nuttiness to the Eagle Rare. Eagle Rare also lingers longer on the palate.

Travel Advice

Buffalo Trace is only a few minutes' drive from downtown Frankfort. It is about an hour from Louisville and forty-five minutes from Lexington. The most direct route from either city is to take the US 127 exit north from I-64 and drive just under five miles into downtown Frankfort. Take a left in front of the Capital Plaza Hotel, which will put you on Wilkinson Boulevard. Drive about a mile, and you will see Buffalo Trace on your left.

It is possible to combine a visit to Buffalo Trace with a visit to the Four Roses or Wild Turkey distillery (or both); each is about half an hour south on US 127. Or you could visit Woodford Reserve, also about thirty minutes from Buffalo Trace via US 60 into Frankfort. But be aware of opening, closing, and tour times to get the most out of your visits.

Nearby Attractions

The attractions, restaurants, and shopping in nearby Frankfort are detailed starting on page 62.

The charming town of Midway (see page 87), with several fine restaurants and shops, is about thirty minutes southeast of Frankfort.

The historic town of Shelbyville is half an hour west of Frankfort on US 60 (or I-64). It is a favorite destination to enjoy browsing the heirloom-quality English and American antique furniture and silver at the **Wakefield-Scearce Antiques Gallery** (http://www.wakefieldscearce.com). (Yes, you can purchase an authentic sterling silver mint julep cup and even have it engraved, but it will *not* be inexpensive.) Located in the beautiful red-brick Georgian building that once housed Science Hill, a girls' school that operated from 1825 to 1939, the complex also includes a number of upscale shops and the **Science Hill Inn** (502-633-2825, http://www.sciencehillinnky.com), serving traditional southern fare in an elegant dining room. Consider spending the morning browsing the shops and having lunch at the inn (you'll probably need a reservation) before heading to Buffalo Trace for an afternoon of distillery touring.

Woodford Reserve Distillery

7855 McCracken Pike
Versailles, KY 40383
859-879-1812
http://www.woodfordreserve.com

Hours: Tuesday–Saturday, 9 a.m.–5 p.m.; Sunday, 12:30–4 p.m. Tours start on the hour beginning at 10 a.m. during the week and 1 p.m. on Sundays. The last tour every day starts at 3 p.m. Closed on major holidays and on Sundays from January through March. There is an admission charge.

Bourbons: Woodford Reserve Distiller's Select, Woodford Reserve Double Oaked, and an annually released limited-edition whiskey in the Master's Collection

Chief Executive: Paul Varga

Master Distiller: Chris Morris

Owner/Parent Company: Brown-Forman Corporation

Tours: The standard Bourbon Discovery Tour ($7) is offered several times daily. Two special tours, the Corn to Cork Tour and the Historic Preservation Tour (each $25), are offered Tuesday through Thursday by reservation and are limited to a handful of visitors.

What's Special:
• The seventy-eight-acre distillery, nestled by the banks of Glenn's Creek, is a National Historic Landmark.
• It has the only stone warehouse in use today for aging bourbon.

- The route to the distillery winds through Kentucky's famous bluegrass horse farms, with bright green pastures populated by grazing Thoroughbreds.
- Whiskey was first distilled on this site in 1812.
- Woodford Reserve is the only triple-distilled bourbon.
- Woodford's three copper pot stills were custom-made by Forsyths of Rothes, Scotland.
- The distillery has a resident chef. Ouita Michel has been nominated for the James Beard Award and is the chef-owner of Holly Hill Inn in nearby Midway.
- A winter holiday lunch buffet is offered in the Dryer House Conference Center from late November through mid-December.
- Several times a year, master distiller Chris Morris conducts a daylong Bourbon Academy, providing an overview of the history and techniques of bourbon making.

History

What is today the Woodford Reserve Distillery traces its roots to a farmer-distiller named Elijah Pepper from South Carolina. Pepper started making whiskey when he arrived in nearby Versailles (the locals pronounce it *ver-sales*) in 1776. Thanks to Pepper's thriving business, he was one of the few farmers who could pay the infamous post–Revolutionary War tax on alcohol, which ignited Pennsylvania's Whiskey Rebellion of 1794. Pepper could also afford to buy 300 acres along the spring-fed Glenn's Creek, a few miles south of Versailles, where he started growing grain and distilling in 1812.

When Pepper died in the early 1830s, his son Oscar inherited the business and built the Old Oscar Pepper Distillery (two stone walls survive from this time). Oscar then made an inspired decision when he hired Dr. James Crow as his distiller. Crow was a Scottish physician and chemist credited with applying standardized scientific techniques to American whiskey making—what we would call "quality control" today. Crow measured the acidity of the distiller's beer produced in the fermenters prior to distillation and used a saccharimeter to track sugar levels throughout the production process. He also measured temperatures at all stages of whiskey making and kept careful records so that he could replicate optimal conditions. But most important, he is credited with being the first to use the sour-mash method, which is still an industry standard. In this technique, a portion of the spent mash from one fermentation is kept back (the "backset") and used as a starter in the next fermentation. This means that the yeast culture is the same each time, and flavors are consistent (think sourdough bread starter).

As people file into the Visitors Center, distillery cat Elijah heads back to his warehouse home.

Crow also used a grain recipe that was three-quarters corn, and he aged his whiskey in charred oak barrels. Sound familiar? The whiskey produced at Old Oscar Pepper probably tasted more like modern bourbon than any of its predecessors. Whiskey made by Crow was sold as Old Pepper and Old Crow.

Oscar Pepper died in 1867 without a will, so his property passed to his wife. Their son James sued his mother for the distillery and won, but he managed to drive it into bankruptcy. Among his bad business decisions was to sell the popular Old Crow brand to E. H. Taylor (bad for Pepper, but good for Taylor). James then moved to New York City (a member of Louisville's Pendennis Club, he is said to have introduced the old-fashioned cocktail to Manhattan).

By the late 1870s, Pepper was forced to sell the distillery to James Graham, who then sold a portion to Frenchman Leopold Labrot. It was called Labrot & Graham Distillery until it was sold to Brown-Forman in 1940. Ironically, Brown-Forman sold the distillery when bourbon popularity declined in the 1970s, only to buy it back in 1994, when bourbon was back in demand. The company spent millions of dollars on restoration and reopened the picturesque facility that now makes Woodford Reserve.

The Tours

The distillery offers three tours, all of which include the distillery, the warehouse, and the bottling room, but two have some added features. Each begins and ends in the Visitors Center, where tickets are purchased (be sure to retain your ticket, which you'll need to get your end-of-tour samples).

The Visitors Center also contains a small but very informative exhibit on bourbon making, a gift shop, and a counter selling gourmet sandwiches and soft drinks (try Ale-8, a soft drink made in Winchester, Kentucky, that is both sweeter and more gingery than ginger ale). On nice days, you can lunch on the deck, which is furnished with wrought iron tables and chairs and overlooks the distillery. You are also invited to use the rocking chairs on the veranda to sit and savor your sample bourbon and bourbon balls after your tour.

The Bourbon Discovery Tour

This hour-long tour is the one most people take, and it is offered several times a day. It begins with a short history film in the Visitors Center, after which a bus takes the tour group down the hill to the distillery proper. You enter the multilevel distillery on the ground floor, where there are samples of the grains used to make the bourbon. Perhaps as a nod to Dr. Crow's attention to detail, all the corn has come from the same farm in nearby Shelby County since the distillery reopened.

A climb up wide oak steps brings you to the mash cooker and the four 7,500-gallon cypress wood fermenters (there is a small elevator for handicapped accessibility). You can tell which one has been active the least amount of time: it is the one producing millions of tiny bubbles and giving off heat. A batch that is nearly ready has only a few large bubbles and feels tepid when you hold your hand over it. The tour then moves into the distilling room, containing Woodford's three sixteen-foot-tall copper pot stills and the multichamber still safe, which is used to monitor the distillate in each.

After an explanation of Woodford Reserve's unique (to bourbon) triple-distillation process, the tour goes back downstairs to a corner of the room devoted to barrels for a discussion of how aging in charred oak affects flavor. In the background is a wall made from used barrel staves; attached to it is a large, handsome plaque with the names of organizations (mostly resorts, hotels, and restaurants) and individuals who have purchased their own barrels of Woodford Reserve. (For details about how to do this, go to http://www.woodfordreserve.com/Bourbon/PersonalSelection.)

A tour enters the steam-heated stone warehouse.

This is the same area where barrels are filled with finished new whiskey and rolled outside, where gravity pulls them along a narrow track to the warehouse. As your group walks across the property to the warehouse, you may see an elderly, very mellow orange and white tabby cat. Elijah wandered onto the property a few years after the distillery reopened, and he apparently spends a lot of time inhaling the evaporating bourbon.

Only one of the three stone warehouses on the property is used for aging bourbon. It is equipped with steam heat, which allows more exact control of the aging cycles than if it were left to the whims of weather. The other two warehouses have been converted into the bottling plant and the shipping and receiving facility.

The Corn to Cork and the Historic Preservation Tours

Each of these tours lasts about two hours and covers all the information in the Bourbon Discovery Tour, but with a lot more detail. If you are interested in all the nitty-gritty of the distilling process—from the grade of field corn used to the alcohol content of the liquid at each step of production—take the Corn to Cork Tour. It is limited to eight people because it includes a visit to the small quality-control lab. There, your guide will give you a taste of the distiller's beer, then add it to a flask and put it in a miniature still. In a few minutes, clear liquid will start to

Enjoying a tasting with friends.

drip into a beaker, and you'll be able to smell and taste the result. The tour is usually offered at 9:30 on Tuesday, Wednesday, and Thursday mornings.

Also offered on Tuesday, Wednesday, and Thursday mornings, but starting at 11:30, is the Historic Preservation Tour. It delves more deeply into the history of the site and the people involved in making whiskey there for the past two centuries. Again, this tour is limited to a slightly smaller group than goes on the general tour, and several additional buildings are visited. A walk along Glenn's Creek is one of the highlights.

The Bourbon

Woodford Reserve Distiller's Select is bottled at 90.4 proof. The mash bill is 72 percent corn, 18 percent rye, and 10 percent malted barley. This is the same recipe used for Brown-Forman's Old Forester, produced in Louisville. In fact, the first release of Woodford Reserve in 1996 actually consisted of "honey barrels" of Old Forester selected by the master distiller and mingled. Some select Old Forester is still used today in batching Woodford Reserve, a practice the distillery does not make secret. Woodford Reserve's propriety yeast strain is kept in the Brown-Forman labs in Louisville; yeast is sent to Woodford as needed, frozen in a culture tube, and propagated on-site.

Frankfort and Midway

Copper pot stills.

Bourbon cocktails about to be poured.

Distiller's Select is aged an average of seven years and four months. All batches are from several barrels, so some of the bourbon used in a bottling may be as young as six or as old as nine years. In the glass, it has a beautiful dark amber or copper color and a rich caramel-vanilla nose, supported by lots of dark fruit (orange peel, dried apricot) and lots of spiciness. All these aromas blend in the mouth in a complex, rich bourbon with a long, smooth finish. This is what you'll sample at the end of your tour.

The Woodford Reserve Double Oaked (available in the gift shop) was released in 2012. It is Distiller's Select that has been put into a heavily toasted and lightly charred second barrel and allowed to age for an extra six to nine months.

Each year since 2005, Woodford Reserve has released a limited-edition Master's Collection whiskey. These have included a Four-Grain (corn, rye, wheat, barley) Maple Wood Finish and a rye packaged and sold as two 350-milliliter bottles instead of a single 750-milliliter one—one bottle finished in new oak barrels and the other in used oak barrels.

I was lucky enough to preview the planned 2019 Master's Collection release—Chocolate Rye Bourbon. I happened to be on-site one day in 2012 when the mash was being fermented, and Chris Morris was on hand to tell me that the rye used in the mash bill had been double-roasted for a chocolaty flavor. I was treated to a taste of the fermenting mash, which did indeed have a strong resemblance to a chocolate shake.

Travel Advice

Woodford Reserve is about an hour from Louisville (going east on I-64), about fifteen minutes from Frankfort (east on I-64 or south on US 60), and thirty minutes from Lexington (going west on I-64 or north on US 60).

From I-64, take the Frankfort/Versailles exit, which is US 60. Turn south (toward Versailles) and drive about two and a half miles to Grassy Springs Road (KY 3360), where you will see a sign for the distillery. Turn right and follow Grassy Springs as it meanders through the horse farms, until it ends at McCracken Pike. Make a right turn, and the distillery is a few hundred yards on the left.

Old Taylor and Old Crow Distilleries

If you have time, there's some bourbon archaeology not far from Woodford Reserve. As you leave Woodford Reserve, turn right and follow the road for about three miles through the town of Millville. On your left, you will see an abandoned building that looks like a small stone and brick castle. This is the "Castle Distillery" that E. H. Taylor Jr. built in

Holiday decoration at Woodford Reserve.

A typical sight along Grassy Springs Road on the way to Woodford Reserve.

1887. Taylor also made bourbon at what is now Buffalo Trace, but he has an even more important place in bourbon history.

In the 1890s whiskey dealers would purchase barrels of whiskey from distilleries, dilute it with water, "enhance" the flavor with a variety of additives that had no business being in bourbon (would you believe tea?!), and then sell it to an unsuspecting public. Naturally, this outraged Taylor and other distillers, who hated the damage that was being done to bourbon's reputation. Taylor contacted John G. Carlisle, Grover Cleveland's secretary of the treasury, and the two men lobbied Congress to pass a bill to protect whiskey quality. The result was the Bottled-in-Bond Act of 1897, which guaranteed that any whiskey sold in a bottle sealed with a government stamp contained nothing but unadulterated straight whiskey that had aged for at least four years and was 100 proof.

When Taylor bought the Old Crow brand from James Pepper, he distilled it at the Old Crow Distillery, which he built in 1872 and is next door to the Castle. Sadly, no distilling takes place in either facility now. In the winter, when the greenery on the chain-link fence surrounding the Old Taylor property has died back, you can just glimpse the columned pavilion, modeled after a Roman bath, that sheltered the distillery's spring.

Beam Global owns Old Crow and still uses the warehouses to age its product, so you may see some Jim Beam trucks coming and going. Beam also makes an 80-proof Old Crow at its Claremont Distillery, but the only thing about this bourbon that its creator would recognize is its name.

Old Frankfort Pike and Midway

Many visitors to Woodford Reserve spend the morning at the distillery and the afternoon driving through the beautiful Bluegrass countryside. Buffalo Trace Distillery in Frankfort is not far away if you want to visit a second distillery.

Drive back along Grassy Springs Road and turn left onto US 60. After about two miles, you'll see Old Frankfort Pike (KY 1681) on the right. Follow it for thirteen rolling, scenic miles. The route is lined with dry-stacked stone walls and board fencing, with horse pastures just beyond, and it is overhung by a canopy of old trees. The **Wallace Station Deli & Bakery** (3854 Old Frankfort Pike, Versailles, 859-846-5161, http://www.wallacestation.com) is housed in an old train station on the left side of the road. Its fresh sandwiches, soups, and baked goods are popular not only with tourists but also with horse farm personnel.

The remains of the Old Taylor Distillery in Millville.

View from Grassy Springs Road in early spring on the way to Woodford Reserve.

Horses aren't the only quadrupeds to be seen along Old Frankfort Pike.

Wallace Station.

One of the most unusual museums in the country is less than five miles east along the road from Wallace Station. **The Headley-Whitney Museum** (4435 Old Frankfort Pike, Lexington, 859-255-6653, http://headley-whitney.org), dedicated to decorative arts, was founded by jewelry designer George W. Headley III and is located on what used to be his family's farm. Exhibits include minutely detailed dollhouses replicating the Cornelius Vanderbilt Whitney estate, a Jewel Room housing many of Headley's creations, a Library, and a Shell Grotto.

After a visit to the museum, drive back west past Wallace Station to US 62 (Midway Road). Turn right, and the route will take you into the little town of Midway, where there's a railroad track down the middle of nineteenth-century Main Street, which is lined with shops and restaurants (Bistro La Belle and Heirloom are highly recommended). A few blocks from the town center, you'll find the **Holly Hill Inn** (426 North Winter Street, 859-846-4732, http://www.hollyhillinn.com), an award-winning restaurant owned by chef Ouita Michel and her husband, Chris.

Also located in Midway are **Equus Run Vineyards** (1280 Moores Mill Road, 859-846-9463 or 877-905-2675, http://www.equusrunvineyards .com), if you're interested in some non-bourbon libations, and the

*Dollhouse at the Headley-
Whitney Museum.*

*Mask of Bacchus by George
Headley.*

Scottwood Bed and Breakfast (2004 Leestown Pike, 877-477-0778,
http://scottwoodbedandbreakfast.com/), with a house that dates from
1795.

For more information about Midway, call 859-846-4413 or go to
http://meetmeinmidway.com.

Enjoying lunch on the patio of the Holly Hill Inn in Midway.

Barrels and Cooperages

When clear new whiskey comes off its final distillation, it is not yet bourbon. That transformation takes place in brand-new oak barrels made by skilled coopers. (By the way, the word *cooper* comes from the medieval Latin *copa*, meaning tun or barrel.) The interiors are burned with an open flame for several seconds to create a charred layer. The new whiskey's alcohol percentage is lowered by adding distilled water, since it cannot go into the barrel at greater than 125 proof. Once the whiskey is in the barrel, it is stored there for several years. During that time, as the whiskey leeches in and out of the cracks in the charred wood, it becomes bourbon and takes on the characteristic amber color and notes of caramel and vanilla. Distillers will tell you that more than half the flavor of bourbon comes from this aging process.

Almost all the barrels used for bourbon made in Kentucky come from two cooperages. Brown-Forman Cooperage is located in Louisville (Brown-Forman is the only distillery in the world that owns its own cooperage). It makes the barrels for Old Forester, Early Times, and Woodford Reserve bourbons, as well as the barrels used at the Jack Daniel's Tennessee whiskey distillery, which is also owned by Brown-Forman. Kentucky Cooperage in Lebanon, Kentucky, is owned by Independent Stave Company, headquartered in (coincidentally) Lebanon, Missouri.

It makes the barrels for virtually all the other bourbon distilleries, as well as custom barrels and casks for microdistillers and barrels for the wine industry.

Here's some barrel trivia: When you are touring a warehouse, look at the heads of paired rivets on a barrel. If they have the letters KY, the barrel was made in Kentucky; MO means it was made in Missouri. (If you see a barrel with BC on the rivets, that doesn't mean it is more than 2,000 years old. Brown-Forman's facility used to be called Bluegrass Cooperage.)

The barrels used for aging bourbon hold fifty-three gallons. Empty, each weighs about 100 pounds; filled

Barrels being charred at Brown-Forman Cooperage.

A cooper raising a barrel at Kentucky Cooperage.

proper shape. A cooper assembles, or "raises," a barrel by hand, choosing the staves that best fit together and placing them within two temporary steel hoops that approximate the position of the lowest of the six hoops that will eventually hold the barrel together. An experienced cooper can raise a barrel every few minutes. The barrels then pass along stations where the wood is steamed to soften it, steel nooses are used to pull the staves together tightly, and more temporary hoops are added.

The most dramatic part of the process is the charring. Historically, this was done by filling barrels with straw and setting the straw on fire. Today, charring is done with gas-fired burners that act as customized flamethrowers. There are four levels of char—number 1 (lightest) to number 4 (darkest)—depending on how long the interior of the barrel is burned. Most bourbon makers use a number 3 char. Wild Turkey, Jim Beam, and Willett prefer number 4. After charring, the barrel heads and bottoms are added, as are the permanent hoops. The bunghole is drilled, and the barrels are shipped to their respective distilleries.

You can watch the steps in this process on tours of the two cooperages, where you will be required to use ear and eye protection and wear close-toed shoes. At Brown-Forman, you weave your way through the cooperage floor for a close-up view of the machinery, much of which was converted for barrel making from the factory's original purpose—producing airplane wings during World War II. Tours of the Brown-Forman Cooperage can be

with new whiskey, they weigh five times that much. During the first year of aging, evaporation (known as the "angels' share") results in the loss of as much as 10 percent of the initial volume. The rate of evaporation is about 4 to 6 percent annually for each subsequent year. Since more water than alcohol evaporates (water is the smaller molecule), the alcohol volume in the barrel becomes more concentrated.

Making barrels requires a combination of highly skilled hand craftsmanship and worker-operated machinery. No glue or nails can be used, since they could introduce contaminants and affect the taste of the whiskey. Staves are milled from air-dried oak to precise specifications. The staves are then lightly heated (toasted) and bent to the arranged only through Mint Julep Tours (to do so, call 502-583-1433 or e-mail Info@MintJulepTours.com). The price includes a very good driving tour of Louisville, with famous landmarks such as Churchill Downs.

At Kentucky Cooperage, visitors are directed to a series of viewing stations. The tours, which are free, begin at 9:30 a.m. and 1 p.m. Monday through Friday. Because of the summer heat, the plant doesn't operate during the first two weeks of July (and sometimes on other days, depending on the temperature). Video tours are available on those days. For more information, go to http://www.independentstavecompany.com/tours. To book a tour, call 270-692-4518.

The barrels can be used only once for bourbon, but that doesn't mean the wood is scrapped after the bourbon is dumped. Used barrels are sold to craft brewers, who use them to finish bourbon-scented ales. Most of the whiskey aged in Scotland is resting in used bourbon barrels. That is also the case for many cognacs, tequilas, and rums.

Many distilleries also sell used barrels to individuals. Look around Kentucky, and you'll see recycled bourbon barrels being used to collect rain from downspouts, as litter receptacles, and—sawn in half—as planters. An empty barrel usually sells for $80 to $100. You can also buy your own full barrel, but that's a bit more expensive.

Most distilleries have a personal or private barrel selection program. Hotels, liquor retailers, and restaurants are the usual purchasers, but individuals or groups willing to spend the money can buy a barrel and have it bottled and labeled with their own name or the name of their organization. The procedure varies a little from distillery to distillery, but generally six to ten barrels are chosen by the master distiller, who may be on hand for your selection, and the purchasers taste from each barrel. You can select a single barrel or choose a couple of barrels to be mingled to obtain the flavor profile you want, which depends on the bourbon's brand and expression. The cost can range from $4,000 to $10,000 or more, based on which bourbon you choose and what volume of bourbon is left in the barrel after aging. And yes, the price includes the empty barrel, too.

The rivets indicate that this barrel was made in Kentucky.

4. Lexington and Horse Country

Town Branch

Lexington calls itself the Horse Capital of the World, and it has every right to do so. The countryside surrounding the city is home to nearly 500 Thoroughbred and Standardbred farms. Keeneland Race Course is the site not only of racing meets held in the spring and fall but also of four yearly horse sales, including the world's largest auction of yearlings. And in addition to welcoming visitors to its museum exhibits and horse demonstrations, the Kentucky Horse Park is a venue for major national and international equestrian events.

Although no one knows exactly how many thousands of horses live in the Bluegrass region, the human population of the Greater Lexington area is about 550,000. At a little more than half the size of the Greater Louisville area, Lexington is Kentucky's second largest city.

The city's history dates to 1775, when a group of frontiersmen from Pennsylvania led by William McConnell established a streamside camp. They received a report from nearby Fort Boonesborough that the war

Nineteenth-century facades on North Broadway in downtown Lexington.

Sunrise at a horse farm near Lexington.

against the British had begun with a battle at Lexington, Massachusetts. So they named their frontier camp Lexington, in honor of the Revolution.

Lexington and surrounding Fayette County have many natural springs and a network of tributary streams to the Kentucky River. With this ready supply of fresh limestone water, several commercial distillers (in addition to all the farmers with stills) were operating in and around Lexington by the early 1780s. Among them was Thomas Lincoln, Abraham Lincoln's great-uncle.

By the middle of the nineteenth century, a Distillery District was developing near the railroad tracks on the northwest side of the city, in the area along today's Manchester Street. Among these were the Turner, Clay & Company Distillery (which eventually became the Ashland Distillery) and the Lexington Distillery, both situated on Town Branch, a tributary of Elkhorn Creek. The most famous of the Lexington distilleries was the James E. Pepper Distillery, which occupied the site of another distillery built in 1858. Colonel James E. Pepper (son of Oscar Pepper, who owned the distillery near Versailles that is now Woodford Reserve) bought the property in 1879, built a new plant, and established the Henry Clay Distillery. The James E. Pepper Distillery, as it was renamed in 1886, was one of the few facilities licensed to make medicinal whiskey during Prohibition. After repeal, Schenley bought the facility and continued to make several brands, including James E. Pepper, Henry Clay, and Indian Hill, until the distillery closed in 1958.

Distillery District

Much as Louisville has promoted the revitalization of its Main Street in recent years, Lexington's Distillery District is undergoing redevelopment. Plans are under way to use the surviving buildings from the Ashland and James E. Pepper distilleries as housing, retail space, and restaurants. Since the district is within a few hundred yards of downtown Lexington and the Rupp Arena (the venue for University of Kentucky basketball games, as well as concerts and other events), city planners have identified a great potential for growth there. A sculptor's studio is already housed in one corner of a Pepper distillery building, which is undergoing extensive renovation. A dinner train will use the track by the distillery as it travels from downtown Lexington to Midway or Frankfort. And the city is constructing a public hiking trail along Town Branch, the stream that runs behind the distillery.

Distillers have started to move back into the neighborhood, too. In 2010 **Barrel House Distillery** (1200 Manchester Street, 859-259-0159, http://barrelhousedistillery.com/) started making Oak Rum (aged in used bourbon barrels), Pure Blue Vodka, and a new whiskey dubbed Devil John Moonshine No. 9. The distillery is open for tours and tastings on Thursdays and Fridays from noon until 5 p.m. and Saturdays and Sundays from 11 a.m. to 3 p.m.

The biggest business at the center of the district's activity is Alltech's Lexington Brewery and Town Branch Distillery.

Town Branch Distillery

> 401 Cross Street
> Lexington, KY 40601
> 859-255-2337
> http://www.lyonsspirits.com/

Hours: Monday–Saturday, 10 a.m.–4 p.m.; Sunday, noon–4 p.m. Tours are year-round and start on the hour. The last tour starts at 3 p.m.
Bourbon: Town Branch
Other Liquors: Pearse Lyons Reserve Malt Whiskey, Bluegrass Sundown (coffee infused with bourbon and sugar), Kentucky Ale, Kentucky Light, Kentucky Bourbon Barrel Ale
Chief Executive: Pearse Lyons
Master Distiller: Roy Court

Exterior of Town Branch Distillery.

Owner/Parent Company: Alltech Lexington Brewing and Distilling
   Company
Tour: The tour includes both the brewery and the distillery. There is a
   $5 admission charge.
What's Special:
- Alltech is one of only a few combined brewing and distilling operations
  in the United States.
- Town Branch is the first new distillery built in Lexington for nearly a
  century.
- It produces the first malt whiskey made in Kentucky since 1919.
- Chief executive Pearse Lyons is originally from Ireland, and master
  distiller Roy Court is from Scotland, as are the copper pot stills used to
  make the whiskies.

History

Chief executive Pearse Lyons is a native of Dublin, Ireland. Although
he worked at Guinness and has university degrees in brewing, including a PhD in yeast fermentation, he didn't start out making beverage
alcohol. Alltech, which he founded in 1980, is a biotechnology company

Interior of Town Branch Distillery.

that specializes in making nutritional supplements for animal feed. Today it has more than 2,500 employees and is one of Lexington's (and Kentucky's) most generous corporate sponsors of sporting and cultural events.

Lyons started Alltech's brewing arm in 2000. Lexington Brewing makes a trio of beers: Kentucky Ale, Kentucky Light, and Bourbon Barrel Ale, aged for six weeks in used bourbon barrels. When he decided to get into the whiskey business, Lyons hired Scottish distiller Roy Court, and Pearse Lyons Reserve Malt Whiskey was released in 2010. Town Branch Bourbon, named for the stream that supplied water to Lexington's earliest distilleries, followed in 2011.

The Tour

The tour begins and ends at the Visitors Center, a building that originally housed the Lexington Ice Company. A short historical video introduces visitors to the history of brewing in Lexington, so this tour is of interest to beer aficionados as well as bourbon lovers. There's a short stop at the Alltech Lexington Brewing Company, located just across the narrow street, where the guide describes the 1950s-era bottling equipment. Fourteen employees are required to staff the line.

The distillery proper was completed in 2012 and opened for tours in

October of that year. Visitors enter through wooden doors decorated with a lion's head door knocker, a whimsical nod to owner Lyons's name. Other architectural flourishes include shutters sporting silhouette cutouts of pot stills and a miniature pot still atop the building's weather vane. This a small enough operation that the mash tubs, fermenters, and stills are all contained in one spacious room with three floor-to-ceiling glass walls. The fourth wall provides a contrast of warm, handsome stone masonry. Both Town Branch Bourbon and Pearse Lyons Reserve Malt Whiskey are distilled in a pair of copper pot stills, made to Alltech's specifications by Forsyths of Rothes, Scotland (the same company that made Woodford Reserve's copper pot stills).

As it comes off the second still, the new whiskey is piped into another room containing the spirits receiver; from there, it is put into barrels. The barrels are taken to Bardstown for aging and are then returned to Lexington for bottling.

Before leaving the distillery, visitors are offered a taste of Town Branch and then escorted back to the Visitors Center gift shop. The colorful shop looks like a re-creation of pub row in Dublin. The "windows" of the pub facade contain shelves for the merchandise, which includes glassware, logo-embossed clothing, beer six-packs, and even Kentucky Ale pub towels—a more British or Irish item than an American one.

The Bourbon

Town Branch is unusual among bourbons, in that it uses nearly as much malted barley as rye. The mash bill is 72 percent corn, 13 percent malted barley, and 15 percent rye. Bottled at 80 proof, the whiskey is aged for three years. The color is a light amber-gold, and there's a good deal of corn and butterscotch in both the nose and the taste. It has a short, sweet finish with a hint of cherry.

Ashland: The Henry Clay Estate

Henry Clay (1777–1852) was one of America's greatest statesmen. He was secretary of state under John Quincy Adams and served as both a U.S. senator and representative from Kentucky, including three terms as Speaker of the House. Clay earned the nickname the Great Compromiser for his role in the legislation that resulted in the Missouri Compromise and the Compromise of 1850, both of which limited the expansion of slavery. Clay, who ran for president several times, was also famous for saying, "I'd rather be right than be president." Of course, he was never president, but you might agree that he was certainly right about his choice of libation: Clay was a famous bourbon lover.

The front of Ashland, Henry Clay's Lexington estate.

Clay's bourbon of choice was Old Crow, a preference that one twentieth-century owner of the label (National Distillers) exploited in a series of print ads showing notable Americans purchasing or drinking Dr. James Crow's whiskey (others included Mark Twain, Buffalo Bill Cody, and Walt Whitman). It is said that Clay enjoyed his bourbon so much that it inspired him to jump up and dance on his banquet table. Although no footmarks can be seen on said table during a tour of Ashland today, it makes a great mental image. The eighteen-room mansion at 120 Sycamore Road, just off Richmond Road, is situated on twenty acres and only a few minutes' drive from downtown. Both the house and the gardens are beautifully preserved. For more information, call 859-266-8581 or go to http://www.henryclay.org.

The Kentucky Horse Park and Horse Farm Tours

As you drive into Lexington from almost any direction, including on the interstate highways, you will see manicured, fence-lined pastures containing graceful, grazing Thoroughbreds. Many visitors to bourbon country also use their time here to get acquainted with Kentucky's horse country. For an excellent introduction to horses in general, as well as to the racing Thoroughbreds, visit the **Kentucky Horse Park** (4089 Iron Works Pike [just off I-75], 859-233-4303 or 800-678-8813, http://www.kyhorsepark.com), only a few minutes' drive from downtown Lexington.

The 1,200-acre park has a state-of-the-art facility for dressage and eventing competitions. The annual Rolex Three Day Event is held there

Old Crow magazine ad from the 1950s.

Shaun Washington looks on as a visitor meets a Thoroughbred in a Keeneland barn.

every spring. The year 2010 marked the first time the prestigious World Equestrian Games were held outside of Europe, and the Kentucky Horse Park hosted them (the main corporate sponsor was Lexington's Alltech).

The park is also home to many horses of many different breeds. You may recognize a Palomino, but you will also see such exotic animals as the red-spotted Knabstrupper. Altogether, there are some fifty breeds, ranging in size from miniature ponies (some dogs are bigger!) to massive draft horses such as the Clydesdales and Belgians. Two of the most popular attractions are the daily Parade of Breeds and the Horses of the World Show. Riders are outfitted in appropriate costumes from their horses' native regions, and the horses themselves sport the appropriate tack.

Champion racehorse Cigar and Kentucky Derby winners Funny Cide and Go for Gin are among the residents, and visitors get to see them up close in the Hall of Champions, a small ring where handlers walk the horses. The International Museum of the Horse traces 50 million years of horse evolution and the shared history of horses and humans. One exhibit features an impressive array of wagons and carriages, and another covers the use of horses in war from ancient times to the twentieth century. A separate building houses the American Saddlebred Museum, devoted to the first horse breed developed in the United States, which originated in Kentucky.

Speaking of wagons, draft horses pull trolleys for tours around the park. And there are even trails where you can take to the saddle for an afternoon of leisurely riding. Pony rides are available for children.

If you want to visit some of the nearby horse farms, the park is the departure point for **Unique Horse Farm Tours**. These are conducted by Shaun Washington, who has worked in several capacities in the racing industry and provides a lively narrative about the farms, their owners, and their equine occupants. Tours vary, depending on which farms are open to visitors on a given day, but you may find yourself feeding peppermints to racehorses in the backside barns at Keeneland or visiting mares and newborns in a farm's foaling barn.

In addition to the tours out of the Kentucky Horse Park, two other Lexington-based companies offer horse farm tours: **Bluegrass Tours** (859-252-5744, http://www.bluegrasstours.com), which also has a combination distilleries and horse farm tour, and **Thoroughbred Heritage Horse Farm Tours** (859-260-8687, http://www.seethechampions.com), which concentrates on the horses.

If you are a racing fan, a visit to historic **Keeneland Race Course** (4201 Versailles Road, 859-254-3412 or 800-456-3412, http://keeneland.com) is a must. Meets are held in April and October. Even if there is no racing, you can start the day with breakfast in the track kitchen, which is open to the public. You can rub elbows with trainers, jockeys, and track staff over cooked-to-order eggs, grits, and bacon. Breakfast is served daily starting at 6 a.m.

More Horsepower in Nearby Georgetown

If you enjoyed the Kentucky Horse Park, you may be interested in two other attractions, each about ten minutes from the park in Georgetown.

Old Friends (1841 Paynes Depot Road, 502-863-1775, http://www.oldfriendsequine.org/) is a retirement farm for racehorses. The horses in residence include Eclipse Award winners and others that could not be retired to breeding for one reason or another. Visitors are allowed to interact with the horses. Tours are conducted daily at 10 a.m., 1 p.m., and 3 p.m., except for the winter, when there is only one tour at 11 a.m. on Sundays. Reservations are required.

As the company likes to say, **Toyota Motor Manufacturing Kentucky** (1001 Cherry Blossom Way, 800-866-4485, http://www.toyotageorgetown.com/tour.asp) specializes in a different kind of horsepower. This automobile assembly plant, located two and a half miles from I-75 exit 126, is Toyota's largest outside of Japan. It opened in 1988.

Today it employs several thousand Kentuckians, features an interactive Visitors Center, and offers guided tours of the factory floor via electric trams. One wonders if Toyota's decision to locate in Kentucky might have been influenced by the famous Japanese fondness for bourbon. Certainly, the presence of Toyota executives and engineers from Japan means that Lexington has an abundance of excellent Japanese restaurants. The Visitors Center is open Monday through Friday from 9 a.m. to 4 p.m. Reservations are strongly recommended for the factory tours.

More Lexington Attractions

As you drive around Lexington, you'll notice a series of signs depicting a bright blue horse. Kentucky's famous bluegrass isn't actually blue (although, after a sip or two of bourbon, you might imagine a bluish cast to the intense green of a fresh spring pasture); nor does eating bluegrass turn horses blue. But if it did, they might look just like this one. In reality, the horse is a Photoshopped image of a painting of the great Thoroughbred named Lexington, and he acts as a colorful guidepost to the city's main attractions. The Lexington Convention and Visitors Bureau has dubbed him "Big Lex." Call 800-845-3959 or go to www.visitlex.com for information about the many non-bourbon-related attractions in the area.

Where to Eat and Drink

Lexington has a lively and varied restaurant scene, including many places with an excellent selection of bourbons. The following is only a small sample of the city's restaurants and bars, chosen with the bourbon drinker in mind. Most are located downtown or in neighborhoods on the edge of downtown. Pricing is indicated as follows: $—inexpensive, with most entrees priced at $15 or less; $$—moderate, at $16 to $25; and $$$—expensive, at $26 or higher.

a la lucie—159 North Limestone, 859-252-5277, http://www.alalucie.com/. Southern and continental, $$.

Al's Bar—601 North Limestone, 859-309-2901, http://alsbarlexington.com/. Sandwiches and the like, $.

Azur Restaurant & Patio—3070 Lakecrest Circle (Beaumont Centre), 859-296-1007, http://www.azurrestaurant.com/. New American, $$–$$$.

Bellini's—115 West Main Street, 859-388-9583, http://www.bellinislexington.com/. Italian, $$–$$$.

Bluegrass Tavern—115 Cheapside, 859-389-6664. No food, but more than 180 bourbons.

The Horse & Barrel.

Cheapside Bar & Grill—131 Cheapside, 859-254-0046, http://cheapsidebarandgrill.com/. American, $–$$.

deSha's—101 North Broadway, 859-259-3771, http://deshas.com/Lexington. American, $$.

Dudley's on Short—259 West Short Street, 859-252-1010, http://www.dudleysrestaurant.com/. American, $$–$$$.

The Grey Goose—170 Jefferson Street, 859-233-1500. American, $–$$.

The Horse & Barrel—107 North Broadway, 859-259-3771. English pub, $.

Jonathan at Gratz Park—120 West Second Street, 859-252-4949, http://jagp.info/. American, $$–$$$.

Lynagh's Irish Pub—384 Woodland Avenue, 859-255-1292, http://www.lynaghsirishpub.com/. Pub grub, $.

Malone's Steakhouse—3347 Tates Creek Road, 859-335-6500, http://www.bluegrasshospitality.com/malones/index.html. Steak house, $$–$$$.

Merrick Inn—1074 Merrick Drive, 859-269-5417, http://themerrickinn.com/. Southern, $$.

Nick Ryan's Saloon—157 Jefferson Street, 859-233-7900, http://nickryans.com/. American, $$.

Portofino—249 Main Street, 859-253-9300, http://www.portofinolexington.com/. Italian, $$$.

Skybar—269 West Main Street (penthouse level), 859-368-7900, http://www.skybarlex.com/. Contemporary and sushi, $$.

Stella's Kentucky Deli—143 Jefferson Street, 859-255-3354, http://stellaskentuckydeli.com/. American, $.

Table Three Ten—310 West Short Street, 859-309-3901, http://www.table-three-ten.com/. American, $$.

Tachibana—785 Newtown Court, 859-254-1911, http://www.tachibanarestaurant.com/. Japanese, $–$$.

Tomo Restaurant—848 East High Street, 859-269-9291, http://www.tomolex.com/. Japanese, $$.

The Tulip Bistro & Bar—355 Romany Road , 859-367-6687, http://www.thetulipbistroandbar.com/. $$.

Where to Stay

Lexington is served by most of the major hotel and motel chains, and the latter can be found at many highway interchanges. For bed-and-breakfasts in the area, go to http://www.kentuckybb.com/lexington-kentucky-bed-breakfast.html. Listed here are the larger hotels, some of which are historic, and many of which are pickup points for tour buses. All the hotel bars have a selection of bourbons. Rates listed are the establishment's lowest. Special features and suites cost more, and daily rates can vary, so you will probably be quoted a higher rate, depending on when you want to stay.

Crowne Plaza Lexington, The Campbell House—1375 South Broadway, 859-255-4281 or 800-227-6963, http://www.thecampbellhouse.net. $109.

Gratz Park Inn—120 West Second Street, 859-231-1777 or 800-752-4166, http://www.gratzparkinn.com. $179.

Griffin Gate Marriott Resort & Spa—1800 Newtown Pike (I-75 exit 115), 859-231-5100 or 877-204-8020, http://www.griffingatemarriott.com. $209.

Hilton Lexington Downtown—369 West Vine Street, 859-231-9000 or 877-539-1648, http://www.lexingtondowntown.hilton.com. $189.

The Gratz Park Inn.

Hyatt Regency Lexington—401 High Street, 859-253-1234 or 800-233-1234, http://www.lexington.hyatt.com. $199.

Inn on Broadway—1301 South Broadway, 859-519-2060, http://www.innonbroadwaylex.com. $67.

Also, what has to be one of the most unusual accommodations in the state can be found just off US 60 near Keeneland Race Course. For $195 a night, you can stay at **The Castle Post** (230 Pisgah Pike, Versailles, 859-879-1000, http://www.thecastlepost.com), a replica of a medieval European castle.

The Master Distiller

Dating from the time of Dr. James Crow, many distillers have declared their pride in their bourbons by putting their own names on the labels. Even today, when many distilleries are large businesses or even parts of multinational corporations, many of the most sought-after bourbons bear the names of the distillers who created them—Russell's Reserve (Jimmy and Eddie Russell of Wild Turkey), Parker's Heritage (Parker Beam of Heaven Hill), Booker's (the late Booker Noe of Jim Beam).

So what exactly does a master distiller do? Distilleries employ scores of people who are engaged in monitoring the yeast tubs, fermenters, and stills, not to mention the men and women who make up the tasting panels that check the flavors of new and aging bourbons. But the master distiller is ultimately responsible for ensuring the quality and consistency of a distillery's products and for developing new expressions and brands of bourbon.

Not long ago, I traveled to Four Roses with my friend Mike Veach (archivist at Louisville's Filson Historical Society and a bourbon historian), where we spent a fascinating morning with master distiller Jim Rutledge and quality-control manager Brent Elliott. We started out in a room that most distillery visitors never see: the quality-control lab. With white counters, shelves filled with glasses and beakers, and several scientific instruments, the room feels like a hybrid chemistry lab and kitchen. Labeled sample bottles of new and aged whiskey sit on the shelves and countertops, and a glass-fronted cabinet contains bottles of every Four Roses brand, as well as the brands of several other distilleries.

Jim and Brent have lined up several stemmed glasses containing clear new whiskies. Each is topped with a watch glass, acting as a lid to keep the liquid's aroma from escaping. Four Roses is famous for having ten different bourbon recipes that involve two mash bills and five different yeast strains, and Jim is about to demonstrate the importance of the yeast to Mike and me. Two of the glasses are OBSV and OBSK, meaning that both whiskies have been distilled here in Lawrenceburg (O), both have been made with the B mash bill (60 percent corn, 35 percent rye, 5 percent barley), and both are straight whiskies (S). They differ only in the yeast strain. As Jim explains, the V strain imparts a "delicate fruitiness" to the whiskey, while the K strain is "slightly spicy." Without looking at the labels, Mike and I lift the watch glasses one at a time and nose the whiskey. One indeed has spicy aroma (nutmeg?), and the other is floral (the power of suggestion, given the Four Roses name, or is it really roses?).

We then compare samples of OBSO and OESO recipes. This time, the yeast strain is the same (the O yeast is supposed to lend "rich fruitiness" to the flavor profile), but the mash bills are different. The E mash bill is 75 percent corn, 20 percent rye, and 5 percent barley. Intriguingly, although fruit is apparent in

Four Roses master distiller Jim Rutledge. (Courtesy of Four Roses)

the noses of both, the whiskey with the lighter rye content also has a lighter fruit character.

We spent the better part of two hours smelling and comparing. Eventually, we nosed and tasted various expressions of Four Roses, including a single-barrel bourbon made with one of the recipes we had nosed in a new whiskey. The flavors were still present, but now they were augmented by vanilla and caramel from the time spent in the wood.

Like all master distillers, Jim makes sure the whiskey has the character he wants before it goes into the barrel, and he checks the whiskey periodically as it ages by extracting tiny amounts from the barrels. It is the master distiller who determines when a bourbon has

reached the point where it is ready for bottling.

Part chemist and part artist, a master distiller is also very much an ambassador. Jim (and several other master distillers I asked) told me that he spends about 70 percent of his time traveling to promote his bourbons. He conducts tastings in restaurants and liquor stores not just in Kentucky and the United States but also in other countries, including Japan, where Four Roses is extremely popular.

Even though none of the Four Roses bourbons is named for Jim, his name is printed on the labels of many of the expressions. Even better, Mike and I each left with a Jim Rutledge–signed bottle of Four Roses Single Barrel.

5. Lawrenceburg
Four Roses and Wild Turkey

Incorporated in 1820, Lawrenceburg was named after local tavern owner William Lawrence. Appropriately, Lawrenceburg is home today to not one but two distilleries. Wild Turkey and Four Roses are only a few minutes' drive from each other and are easily reached via US 127 from Frankfort. The Bluegrass Parkway also serves as a conduit from Lexington or Bardstown.

One warning about US 127: During the first week of August every year, 690 miles of the highway from Michigan to Alabama is the site of the World's Longest Yard Sale. Traffic slows to a crawl. Since neither Four Roses nor Wild Turkey makes bourbon in August anyway, this is a good time to avoid the area, unless, of course, you want to bargain hunt. For information about the sale, go to http://www.127sale.com/ or call 800-327-3945.

Four Roses Distillery

> 1224 Bonds Mill Road
> Lawrenceburg, KY 40342
> 502-839-3436
> http://www.fourroses.us

Hours: Monday–Saturday, 9 a.m.–3 p.m.; Sunday, noon–3 p.m. Tours start on the hour and are available year-round, but there is no distilling from July to mid-September. The gift shop is open daily until 4 p.m. Call for tour groups of ten or more. Tours of the Four Roses warehouse and bottling facility at Cox's Creek (about an hour's drive from the distillery) are given Monday–Friday, 9 a.m.–2 p.m. Call 502-543-2264 for information.

Bourbons: Four Roses Yellow Label, Four Roses Single Barrel, Four Roses Single Barrel Limited Edition, Four Roses Small Batch, and Four Roses Small Batch Limited Edition; plus Four Roses Black Label

The US 62 bridge, with Wild Turkey warehouses in the background.

and Four Roses Super Premium ("Platinum"), which are for export only

Chief Executive: Hideki Horiguchi

Master Distiller: Jim Rutledge

Owner/Parent Company: Kiren Brewery Company Ltd.

Tours: There is one standard tour that lasts about an hour. Visitors are given a choice of bourbons to taste at the tour's conclusion. If a Four Roses expression (even a limited edition) is available, the gift shop stocks it for purchase.

What's Special:

- California mission-style architecture is unusual and unexpected in the Bluegrass State and has earned Four Roses a listing on the National Register of Historic Places.
- Bottling and aging take place an hour from the distillery at the Cox's Creek site.
- The warehouses at Cox's Creek are the only single-story warehouses in the bourbon industry.
- A combination of five yeast strains and two mash bills results in ten different bourbon recipes.
- The distillery sponsors a Four Roses Mellow Moments Club, with

Exterior of Four Roses Distillery.

membership perks such as discounts in the gift shop and VIP tours and tastings (www.mellowmomentsclub.com).

History

The bourbon industry in general has numerous legends, from how barrels came to be charred to various claims about who was the first person to distill bourbon. So it isn't surprising that Four Roses Distillery has its own share of lore—in this case, contradictory stories about the origin of the distillery's name.

One version, which appears on the back label of Four Roses 80-proof bourbon, states that Paul Jones Jr., one of the nineteenth-century founders of the brand, was courting "a beautiful Southern belle" and had asked her many times to marry him, but his proposal had always been rejected. Jones decided to make one last attempt and invited her to a dance. He told her that when he arrived to pick her up, if she was wearing a corsage of four roses, her answer to his persistent proposal would be yes. If she wore no roses, there would be no marriage. Her answer was yes! Jones, who was just starting his distilling business in Kentucky, was so delighted that he named his best bourbon after this sign of love.

Alternatively, according to Al Young's very enjoyable *Four Roses: The Return of a Whiskey Legend*, the suitor was Paul Jones Jr.'s cousin and business partner, Lawrence Lavalle Jones. The object of his affection and the wearer of the corsage was indeed a southern belle: Mary Peabody of Columbus, Georgia. Or perhaps this isn't the real story either.

Another version requires some background: The Jones family traced its roots to Virginia, and during the Civil War, Paul Jones Sr. and his two sons, Paul Jr. and Warner Paul, supported the South. Warner Paul enlisted in the Confederate army and, by sheer coincidence, took part in the 1862 Battle of Perryville, Kentucky's most significant Civil War battle, which occurred just thirty miles south of Four Roses' current distillery site. Colonel Warner Paul Jones was subsequently killed in the war. After the conflict ended, other Jones family members relocated to Atlanta, where they became successful in the whiskey business. But in 1883, when a strong temperance movement brought Prohibition to Georgia, the Joneses moved to Tennessee, where they grew their business, acting as brokers for distillers. Attracted by the concentration of bourbon businesses in Louisville, they moved to Kentucky by 1886. Two years later, in 1888 (the year the company cites as its origin), the Joneses bought assets from whiskey maker R. M. Rose, who is said to have named his bourbon after his four daughters. In yet another version of the story, the name was based on Mr. Rose, his brother, and their two sons. Whether it signified sons or daughters, the Joneses acquired the Four Roses name, along with other Rose assets, and operated as the Paul Jones Company.

Paul Jones Jr. continued his bourbon brokerage business, buying thousands of barrels of bourbon, until Prohibition. Jones then managed to acquire one of the half dozen licenses in the country (four of them in Kentucky) to distribute "medicinal" whiskey. Jones moved his stock to Frankfort and opened the Frankfort Distilleries, where he bottled Four Roses, Paul Jones, and Antique bourbons. The Paul Jones Company also acquired an interest in Louisville's A. Ph. Stitzel Distillery so that it could continue to meet the pharmaceutical demand.

Members of the Jones family ran the business until World War II. In 1943 Canadian beverage giant Joseph E. Seagram & Sons Inc. purchased Frankfort Distilleries and four other Kentucky distilleries—Old Hunter Lewis Distillery, Athertonville Distillery, Henry McKenna Distillery, and Old Prentice Distillery. Old Prentice is the 1910 Spanish mission–style facility that Seagram used to make Four Roses and that houses the distillery today. Under Seagram, Four Roses was exported to Europe and Japan, where it became very popular and helped drive the demand for bourbon outside the States. (Ironically, for decades, Four Roses was sold only in America as an inexpensive—and, quite frankly, awful—blended whiskey.)

Acquiring these five Kentucky distilleries is how Seagram wound up

Lawrenceburg

with five distinct strains of yeast. The company also established two mash bills for all five sites: one uses a corn and rye ratio that is fairly typical in the industry, and the other uses a higher proportion of rye (though corn still predominates, of course). Four Roses—the distillery and warehouse, along with the yeast strains and mash bills—was purchased by Kiren Brewery Company of Japan in 2002. The truly good news is that Kiren reintroduced the premium Four Roses bourbons to the American market, and you can taste them at the end of your tour.

The Tour

The bright yellow stucco walls of the Four Roses Distillery complex guarantee that potential visitors can't miss it. From spring through fall, the property is blooming with hundreds of bright red roses and other flowers.

The tour begins with a film that dwells much less on history compared with the orientation films at other distilleries. The emphasis is on the bourbon and how it's made, with narration by master distiller Jim Rutledge. Then the tour guide goes into great detail about the yeast strains and the mash bills, complete with a flip chart. To save you from furious note taking, here are the specifics:

Mash bills: E—75 percent corn, 20 percent rye, 5 percent malted barley
               B—60 percent corn, 35 percent rye, 5 percent malted barley

Yeast strains: V—Light fruitiness
               K—Slightly spicy
               O—Rich fruitiness
               F—Herbal
               Q—Floral

Five recipes are made with mash bill E and each of the yeast strains, and five are made with mash bill B and each of the yeasts, for a total of ten recipes.

The first stop after orientation is the grain quality lab, a small building near the distillery entrance, where each shipment of corn, rye, and barley is evaluated before being milled. Small samples of grain are put into a stemmed glass and microwaved for twenty seconds. This brings out the aromas, making any flaws easier to detect. Four Roses usually receives three truckloads of corn each day and one truckload of rye Monday through Friday; barley is delivered once a week.

Relaxing under one of the distillery's catalpa trees.

*Tanker truck carrying 6,000 gallons of new whiskey prepares
to leave for the bottling facility at Cox's Creek.*

Lawrenceburg

The tour then moves into the main distillery. Although the building is
listed on the National Register of Historic Places, the technology inside
is anything but archaic. A large room just inside the entrance contains
the computerized electronics that control the distilling. A series of
metal stairs takes you to the fermentation room, where red cypress and
stainless steel tanks contain the fermenting sour mash in various stages

(opposite) Interior of the still house.

(left) A fountain in the garden at Four Roses.

(below) A tour group passes barrels bearing the Four Roses logo.

of completion. The guide explains the details of the distillation process, including the percentage of alcohol in the distiller's beer (8 percent, in this case).

One of the rather unusual aspects of the Four Roses process is that aging does not occur at this site (the warehouses across the street actually belong to Wild Turkey). The new whiskey is put into 6,000-gallon tanker trucks and taken to the Four Roses warehousing and bottling facility at Cox's Creek, near Bardstown.

The Bourbon

The tour wraps up with a tasting that gives you a true appreciation of the various Four Roses recipes. You can taste small samples of Yellow Label, Single Barrel, and Small Batch.

The honey-gold Yellow Label is a product of the mingling of all ten Four Roses bourbon recipes. It is bottled at 80 proof, which gives it a light character but also results in a lively bouquet in which fruity notes, including apple and pear, are easily detected. The finish is long and sweet. It is very pleasant sipped neat and is an excellent bourbon for cocktail mixing.

Because of the multiple recipes, the Single Barrel bottles from this distillery are more variable than most single-barrel bourbons. If your guide doesn't mention it, ask about the formula (printed on the label).

A decorative gate with the distillery's symbol.

Rolling out barrels at Cox's Creek.

Depending on which yeast strain was used for the bottle you are tasting from, there may be a stronger presence of fruit or spice (cinnamon is common) or even a floral nose (yes, roses). The higher rye mash bill is always used for Single Barrel.

While many distilleries define "small batch" in numbers of well over a hundred barrels, Four Roses takes the term a bit more to heart. The average number of barrels used for a Small Batch bottling is nineteen. The bourbon's color is polished bronze, and the nose is characterized by chocolate and toffee in balance with the vanilla. As you sip, a series of fruit flavors emerges—from spicy apple through citrus to dark fruit—with a long, rich finish. Interestingly, Small Batch is a product of the mingling of four of the ten recipes.

One more note about the Four Roses recipes: The Single Barrel bottles contain a series of four letters, such as OBSQ. The O stands for the Lawrenceburg distillery (which was important when Seagram had five distilleries), B designates the 60 percent corn mash bill (E would designate the 75 percent corn mash bill), S means that it was made by the straight whiskey-making process, and Q is the yeast strain.

Cox's Creek Tour

There has been so much interest in the Four Roses warehouse that it too is now open for tours, Monday through Friday from 9 a.m. to 2 p.m. To get to the site from the distillery, go back up Bonds Mill Road to US 127 and turn right. About a quarter mile ahead, you will see the signs for the Bluegrass Parkway. Turn right onto the Bluegrass Parkway west (the signs are for Elizabethtown) and drive about thirty-four miles to exit 25, US 150 (Springfield/Bardstown). Turn right on US 50 (Springfield Road), and after just a fifth of a mile, turn right onto KY 245, New Shepherdsville Road. Follow this road for a little over thirteen miles, and you will see the sign for Four Roses on your right. This drive takes a bit less than an hour. Of course, you could simply follow one of the tanker trucks from the distillery, but they tend to leave early in the morning.

Check in at the barrel-shaped guard office to join a tour, which includes a peek in one of the unique one-story warehouses that date from Seagram's ownership. There were originally twenty-one (designated A through U), but Warehouse O had to be demolished due to a construction flaw. Each warehouse sits on its own acre, and the ground has been graded so that it slopes away from each building. (If a fire starts in one warehouse, the burning bourbon will flow downhill and be trapped in

View of the unique one-story warehouses at Cox's Creek.

a depression, keeping the fire from spreading.) In contrast to the many variables in its recipes, Four Roses' one-story warehouses take the variables out of aging. Whereas temperatures in traditional seven-story warehouses can vary as much as thirty-five degrees Fahrenheit from the bottom row of barrels to the top one, there's a maximum of only eight degrees' difference in these warehouses.

At Cox's Creek, you'll also see where the tanker trunks weigh in and discharge their loads for barreling. In the bottling facility, a combination of technology and manual skill is used for filling and labeling.

Cox's Creek is the place you would come to select your own personal barrel of Four Roses. Barrels are brought to a space behind the labeling room, and master distiller Jim Rutledge is often on hand to help with the selection.

The Cox's Creek site covers nearly 300 acres, and Four Roses uses an interesting method to maintain the grounds. You may notice a herd of black-and-white cattle in the distance by the trees. These cattle belong to the distillery and are allowed to graze between the warehouses after hours to keep the grass short.

Travel Advice

The Four Roses Distillery is on Bonds Mill Road, just off US 127, which is about fifteen miles south of I-64 exit 53-A. The distillery is about an hour's drive from downtown Louisville, less than half an hour from Frankfort, about half an hour from downtown Lexington, and forty minutes from Bardstown. Because it's only fifteen minutes away from the Wild Turkey Distillery, many visitors tour both in the same day. You could even take in three distilleries in one day if you tour Four Roses and Wild Turkey in the morning, go to Frankfort for lunch, and tour Buffalo Trace in the afternoon.

If you are interested in the Cox's Creek tour, you might want to combine it with a trip to the Jim Beam Distillery, which is only a five-minute drive west of the warehouses.

Perryville Battlefield State Historic Site

Colonel Warner Paul Jones, whose family founded Four Roses, commanded Confederate troops in the Battle of Perryville, which took place on October 7 and 8, 1862. If you are interested in Civil War history, you might want to visit the battlefield, which is preserved as a 669-acre state park (http://www.parks.ky.gov/findparks/histparks/pb/).

More than forty interpretive signs along self-guided trails vividly re-create the battle, which resulted from a chance encounter between

Union and Confederate troops moving through Kentucky. Nonetheless, Perryville was an important conflict. Many historians believe that if the Confederates had succeeded in capturing Kentucky (which remained in the Union during the Civil War), the South could very well have won the war. As it happened, the 16,000 Confederates were vastly outnumbered at Perryville by 58,000 Union troops—unbeknownst to the commanders at the time. More than 7,500 soldiers were killed or wounded in the battle.

Every October, the battle is reenacted on the weekend closest to its actual dates. For tickets and information, go to http://www .perryvillebattlefield.org.

To get to the park from Four Roses, take US 127 south about fifteen miles to Harrodsburg. This town is Kentucky's oldest permanent settlement, and there is a re-creation of Fort Harrod (http://www.parks. ky.gov/findparks/recparks/fh/) along the way if you want even more Kentucky history. In Harrodsburg, turn right onto Mooreland Avenue (US 68); after a fifth of a mile, Mooreland becomes KY 152 as you bear right. Follow KY 152 for eleven and a half miles, turn left on Deep Creek Road (KY 442), drive about four miles, and follow the signs to the park (1825 Battlefield Road, Perryville, 859-332-8631).

Reenactment of the Battle of Perryville.

Wild Turkey Distillery.

Wild Turkey Distillery

1525 Tyrone Road
Lawrenceburg, KY 40342
502-839-4544
http://www.wildturkeybourbon.com

Hours: Tours are given Monday–Saturday at 9 a.m., 10:30 a.m., 12:30 p.m., 2:30 p.m., and 3:30 p.m. and on Sundays (March–December) at 1 p.m., 2 p.m., and 3 p.m. The gift shop is open 9 a.m.– 4:30 p.m. Monday–Saturday and 12:30–4:30 p.m. on Sunday. Closed on Thanksgiving and Christmas.

Bourbons: Wild Turkey 81, Wild Turkey 101, Russell's Reserve 10-Year-Old, Russell's Reserve Single-Barrel, Wild Turkey Rare Breed, Wild Turkey Kentucky Spirit, Master Distiller's Selection (annually released)

Ryes: Wild Turkey Kentucky Straight Rye, Russell's Reserve 6-Year-Old Rye

Other Liquors: Wild Turkey American Honey Liqueur

Chief Executive: Bob Kunze-Concewitz

Master Distiller: Jimmy Russell

Associate Distiller: Eddie Russell

Owner/Parent Company: Gruppo Campari

Tour: The tour includes the distillery and a warehouse, and visitors are given a choice of several products for tasting.

What's Special:

- The distillery is perched atop a cliff more than 250 feet above the Kentucky River.
- Whiskey was first distilled on this site in 1869.
- The new distillery, which more than doubled the previous capacity, opened in 2011. It was the first new distillery built in the United States since the boom years just after the repeal of Prohibition.
- Wild Turkey is the largest-capacity whiskey distillery in the world.
- Master distiller Jimmy Russell has been with the distillery since 1954.
- Wild Turkey 101 was reportedly the favorite bourbon of both President Dwight D. Eisenhower and gonzo journalist Hunter S. Thompson.

History

Wild Turkey's history is a hybrid of traditional Kentucky bourbon making and the evolution of a New York wholesale grocery company. The first distillery on the current site was built in 1869 and purchased (and rebuilt) by Irish immigrant J. P. Ripy in 1888. Ripy's brands were J. P. Ripy, Old Hickory Club, Old Hickory Spring, Sam Stevens, and J. W. Stevens. In 1906 Ripy's sons became involved in the business, and it was renamed Ripy Brothers Distillery; it produced Ripy Brothers and Old Hardy bourbons until the facility was closed by Prohibition.

In 1937, four years after the end of Prohibition, the Ripys updated the distillery, which was in operation until the present distillery was built. Through the years, the distillery was sold several times and produced several different bourbons, including Old Joe and J. T. S. Brown, though members of the Ripy family continued to be associated with it. When current Wild Turkey master distiller Jimmy Russell started working at the distillery in 1954, one of the people who taught him about bourbon making was distillery manager Ernest W. Ripy.

But part of Wild Turkey's heritage predates the distillery. Austin, Nichols & Company Inc., a food importing and distribution business, was founded in 1855 by Friend P. Fitts, who had made a fortune in the California Gold Rush. After the repeal of Prohibition, Austin Nichols started selling its own spirits, including straight bourbon. By the early 1940s, it was purchasing bourbon from a variety of suppliers, but primarily from Boulevard Distillery—the plant the Ripys had built.

Around this time, Austin Nichols president Thomas McCarthy took some of his company's bourbon along on a turkey hunt with three of his friends. They enjoyed the whiskey so much that McCarthy decided to

Taking a ride on an old barrel that has been converted to a "rocking turkey."

name it after the object of their sport, and the Wild Turkey brand was introduced in 1942.

In 1972 Austin Nichols bought the distillery itself, renamed it Wild Turkey, and made it the exclusive venue for the production of Wild Turkey whiskies. An international element was introduced when Austin Nichols sold the plant and the brands to Pernod Ricard of France in 1980. Today the distillery is owned by the Italian company Gruppo Campari, which purchased it in 2009.

The Tour

Even if you toured Wild Turkey as recently as the spring of 2011, the experience will now be very different. That's because the 1937 Ripy family distillery, where Jimmy Russell perfected his bourbon-making skills, was replaced by a brand-new, gleaming facility that opened in June 2011. The new 134,000-square-foot distillery and offices cost $50 million and more than doubled the production capacity of Wild Turkey, from about 5 million gallons annually to 11 million gallons. And that's not the only change: ground was broken in 2012 on a new $44 million bottling

The 1930s Wild Turkey facility, photographed in 2012. It is scheduled for demolition.

and packaging plant, which is projected to open in the fall of 2013. So every aspect of production—milling the grain, fermentation and distillation, and aging and bottling—will take place on the Lawrenceburg property.

One more big change is coming to Wild Turkey. Depending on the construction schedule, the current Visitors Center, consisting of a little house by the woods, will be replaced with a striking new one in 2013 or 2014. The building will be downhill from the distillery and will boast spectacular panoramic views of the palisades of the Kentucky River. Building materials will be a mixture of historic and modern, including barn siding incorporated into the interior. The reception area will be made of amber-colored glass, and interactive displays will include iPad stations.

The tour of the distillery begins outdoors by the giant grain silos. They overlook a very large, colorful turkey painted on the side of the distillery building—a favorite backdrop for photos. Moving indoors, you'll see a short film about making Wild Turkey narrated by master distiller Jimmy Russell and featuring both the elder Russell and his son, associate distiller Eddie Russell.

(opposite) Wild Turkey warehouse interior.

Distillers Jimmy and Eddie Russell in the tasting lab.

In contrast to the old distillery, which had cypress fermenting tanks arranged in a rather dark, low-ceilinged room, the new facility's stainless steel tanks occupy a bright, high-ceilinged space with walls of windows facing southeast and southwest. The quality-control laboratory is visible through a large window on another wall of the tasting room.

This is where the Russells and other staff evaluate new whiskey that has just come off the still, as well as the aged whiskies prior to bottling. A handy design feature in the tasting lab is that the samples are arranged on a giant lazy Susan–like tabletop, allowing the evaluators to stay seated as they sample each glass in turn and keeping the bottles in the designated order.

Jimmy Russell will tell anyone who asks (and it's not uncommon for tours to encounter him) that the mash bill for all Wild Turkey bourbons is the same, although he won't reveal the exact proportions of the grains. Part of what makes Wild Turkey 81, Wild Turkey 101, Russell's Reserve, and American Spirit distinctive are differences in proof and age.

After viewing the still house, the tour moves to a warehouse, where the guide explains that, unlike some other distilleries, Wild Turkey's warehouses are not climate controlled. Windows are opened in summer and closed in winter.

Kentucky law limits the volume of alcohol that distilleries can offer for sampling, but at the end of the tour, you can choose to sip any two of these six products: Wild Turkey 101, Russell's Reserve 10-Year-Old Bourbon, Wild Turkey Rare Breed, Kentucky Spirit, Russell's Reserve 6-Year-Old Rye, and American Honey, a liqueur made with bourbon.

Tour guides Daniel Pollis and Alan Tenniswood pour tastes.

The Bourbon

Wild Turkey bourbons have a deserved reputation for robustness. The new whiskey off the still is a lower proof than most other bourbons, so less water is added before it is put into barrels with a number 4 char (the darkest) for aging.

Wild Turkey 101 is named for its proof. When Austin Nichols introduced Wild Turkey in 1942, it was aged eight years—about twice as long as most bourbons on the market at the time. You can still buy eight-year-old Wild Turkey with the age printed on the label, but most 101 (and the expression offered in the tasting) is a mingling of variously aged barrels. Deep amber in color, it has a spicy nose and a correspondingly peppery flavor on the tongue, but it finishes with a surprising honey sweetness.

Russell's Reserve 10-Year-Old is a 90-proof, small-batch bottling. To my palate, it has more vanilla character than any of the other Wild Turkey bourbons, and it retains the characteristic Wild Turkey spiciness and nuttiness.

Rare Breed is a mingling of six-, eight-, and twelve-year-old bourbons and is bottled at 108.4 proof. Roasted corn predominates in the nose and on the palate. The finish is long, smooth, and honey scented.

Wild Turkey's single-barrel bourbon is Kentucky Spirit, bottled at 101 proof. The honey here intensifies to honeycomb, and the spice is less peppery and more like nutmeg and cinnamon, with an underlying nuttiness.

If you have never tasted rye, Russell's Reserve 6-Year-Old Rye is an excellent introduction. You'll detect rye in the nose, on the tongue, and at the finish, all with underlying notes of vanilla and a little honey.

Given the distinctive honey notes in the Wild Turkey bourbons, it was natural to use honey in making American Honey Liqueur. If you enjoy Drambuie, you'll love this 71-proof liqueur.

Travel Advice

From I-64, take exit 53-A to US 127 and travel south for about fourteen miles. Just past the Wal-Mart Superstore on your left, turn left onto US 44, which becomes US 62, and travel about two and a half miles before turning right onto Tyrone Road. You'll see the distillery. The Wal-Mart is just over four and a half miles north of the Bluegrass Parkway if you are coming from that direction.

Given Wild Turkey's proximity to Four Roses, you might want to visit both distilleries in one day. You can also enjoy some pretty Kentucky countryside by taking the back roads to Woodford Reserve and thereby indulge in a study of contrasts, comparing the ultramodern Wild Turkey

Metal-clad warehouses on the Wild Turkey property.

facility with Brown-Forman's historic, early-nineteenth-century site. From Wild Turkey, cross the bridge over the Kentucky River on US 62 and follow the highway for three and a half miles. Make a sharp left onto KY 1685/Steele Road and stay on it for five miles; then turn left onto McCracken Pike. Woodford Reserve is about two miles down the road. Travel time is just under half an hour.

Where to Stay

If you want to enjoy some true Kentucky hospitality while visiting the eastern portion of bourbon country, there are two historic accommodations in nearby Harrodsburg, about half an hour's drive south of Lawrenceburg. Both have restaurants specializing in regional cuisine.

Beaumont Inn

You can be forgiven if the theme to *Gone with the Wind* pops into your head when you pull up to the Beaumont Inn (638 Beaumont Inn Drive, Harrodsburg, 859-734-3381 or 800-352-3992, http://www .beaumontinn.com/). It happens to a lot of people. At one time, the antebellum mansion was an exclusive girls' school. Now guests can stay in antiques-appointed rooms and enjoy southern delicacies such as fried chicken, country ham, and corn pudding in the dining room. And yes, you'll find grits on the breakfast menu. The inn complex (there are two other historic buildings for overnight guests) also includes a casual

Beaumont Inn.

Dessert at the Beaumont Inn.

restaurant, the Owl Tavern, and a cozy pub, the Owl's Nest; both feature personalized bourbon tastings. Contact proprietor Dixon Dedman to book one (dixon@beaumontinn.com).

Dixon, his wife Elizabeth, and his parents, Helen and Chuck Dedman, own and run the Beaumont Inn, which has been the family business since 1919, the year the Volstead Act was passed. This is not a coincidence. Before they were innkeepers, the Dedmans were distillers. The tavern and pub at the Beaumont Inn are named in honor of Charles M. Dedman's Kentucky Owl Distillery, which operated thirteen miles north at Oregon, Kentucky, on the Kentucky River. From 1880 until 1916 it produced Kentucky Owl and C. M. Dedman bourbons. Dedman died in 1918, and the advent of Prohibition meant that his distillery never reopened. Large black-and-white photos of the old distillery are part of the tavern's décor.

Shaker Village of Pleasant Hill

The Shakers were a nineteenth-century communal society that promoted racial and gender equality, practiced celibacy, and was renowned for its craftsmanship. The village they established in 1805 and maintained through the nineteenth century at Pleasant Hill has been painstakingly restored, and overnight guests are welcome to stay in fifteen different buildings on the 3,000-acre property. Staff members in Shaker clothing tend farm animals and crops, make implements and furniture, and serve patrons in the Trustees' Office Dining Room.

Shaker Village of Pleasant Hill (3501 Lexington Road, Harrodsburg, 859-734-5411 or 800-734-5611, http://www.shakervillageky.org) is a fine place to relax after spending the day touring bourbon country. In the morning, a buffet breakfast is served, providing fuel for the next day's

An autumn day in Shaker Village.

explorations. The grounds include forty miles of hiking and equestrian trails, including walks along the Kentucky River, and a nature preserve. The restaurant serves traditional Shaker fare (don't pass up the Shaker lemon pie). Bourbon is offered, of course, and twice a year, Shaker Village hosts a bourbon-themed dinner as a fund-raiser for the nonprofit foundation that maintains the site.

Some of the buildings where overnight guests can stay at Shaker Village of Pleasant Hill.

Not Just the Angels' Share

Without a doubt, one of the highlights of a distillery tour occurs in the warehouse, when visitors are enveloped by the rich and luscious aromas of caramel and vanilla rising from the aging barrels. Inhaling is almost, but not quite, as satisfying as sipping the end product. There's a lot of whiskey vapor in the air. In fact, over time, as much as two-thirds of a barrel can evaporate, depending on how long the bourbon is aged. Distillers whimsically refer to this evaporation as the "angels' share." But in reality, the evaporating bourbon is providing nutrition for far more corporeal beings.

During a distillery tour, you may notice that light-colored warehouses and even nearby fences, trees, and concrete walls are streaked with black markings, as if soot had settled on their surfaces. But obviously it can't be soot, since fire is not allowed anywhere in the vicinity of the highly flammable whiskey. (No doubt you will notice the numerous No Smoking signs, too.) The discoloration—known in the industry as warehouse staining—is caused by millions of microscopic fungi growing on the darkened surfaces. It is a species of black mold with the tongue-twisting name *Baudoinia*

compniacensis—commonly known as the whiskey fungus—and it was first described in an 1881 paper published in a French scientific journal. The mold had long been observed staining warehouses where cognac was being aged and on surfaces near bakeries, where rising dough also released ethanol.

Baudoinia happily grows outdoors in the presence of ethanol vapors, but it has proved difficult to culture in a lab. Recently, however, Canadian scientists studied samples taken from concrete walls near rye warehouses in Ontario and from bourbon warehouses in Kentucky and concluded that the same species of mold is responsible for warehouse staining in France, Canada, and the United States. Happily, it doesn't harm trees and seems to have no adverse health effects on people or animals, since we have been co-existing with *Baudoinia* for as long as we have been baking and distilling. And the lofty angels apparently don't mind sharing with the humble little fungi.

Warehouse C at Buffalo Trace, Frankfort, was damaged by a tornado in 2006. The replaced bricks on the top show the effects of staining on the rest of the building.

6. Bardstown

The Kentucky Bourbon Festival, Barton 1792,

Heaven Hill Bourbon Heritage Center, Kentucky

Bourbon Distillers, Maker's Mark, and Jim Beam

Bardstown calls itself the Bourbon Capital of the World, and with good reason. It is home to the Barton 1792 Distillery; headquarters of Heaven Hill Distilleries, along with its bottling plant and warehouses; Kentucky Bourbon Distillers' Willett Distillery; and the Oscar Getz Museum of Whiskey History. Maker's Mark Distillery is about half an hour south of town, and both the Jim Beam Distillery and the Four Roses warehouses and bottling operation are about a twenty-minute drive northwest. As if that weren't enough to lay claim to the name, Bardstown also hosts the Kentucky Bourbon Festival, an annual six-day celebration of the city's most famous product.

In 1780 brothers David and William Bard used a 1,000-acre land grant from Governor Patrick Henry of Virginia to found Bardstown, which is Kentucky's second-oldest town. In addition to being famous for bourbon, Bardstown is the site of the oldest Catholic cathedral west of the Appalachian Mountains (St. Joseph's Proto-Cathedral happens to be just next door to the Oscar Getz Museum of Whiskey History).

Another claim to fame is the Georgian mansion known as Federal Hill, enshrined at **My Old Kentucky Home State Park** (501 East Stephen Foster Avenue, 502-348-3502, http://parks.ky.gov/parks/recreation-parks/old-ky-home/default.aspx). Federal Hill was home to the Rowan family and was reportedly visited by the Rowans' Pittsburgh cousin, composer Stephen Foster, in the 1850s. Inspired by the house and the surrounding plantation, Foster penned the song that would become the state's anthem, sung by tens of thousands of Kentucky Derby spectators the first Saturday in May. The mansion and grounds are open for tours given by guides in period costume. Every summer, *Stephen Foster: The Musical* is performed in the park's amphitheater. In the past, the park grounds served as one of the sites for the Bourbon Festival, and they may do so again. Call or visit the park's website for more information about tours and performances.

The Richardson Romanesque–style Visitors Center was formerly the county courthouse.

Federal Hill at My Old Kentucky Home State Park.

Bardstown itself is a charming place, with more than 300 buildings listed on the National Register of Historic Places. The streets around Courthouse Square are lined with shops, restaurants, and bed-and-breakfasts. And most of the restaurants have an excellent selection of bourbon. Several of the large historic houses along North Third Street constituted what was known as Distillers' Row, since many lived here.

Fred Noe, master distiller for Jim Beam, still lives on the street. For more details on Bardstown's non-bourbon-related attractions and festivals, go to http://www.visitbardstown.com/.

The Kentucky Bourbon Festival

The Kentucky Bourbon Festival began in 1992 with a dinner and tastings. Today it has grown into a six-day event with concerts, races, a golf tournament, a cocktail contest, cooking and drink-mixing classes, expert panel discussions, an auction of bourbon memorabilia, a gala black-tie dinner, and more. In 2011 some 50,000 people attended the festival, traveling from thirty-eight states and fourteen countries.

The center of the festival's activities is the Spalding Hall lawn, just outside the entrance to the Oscar Getz Museum of Whiskey History (114 North Fifth Street). Almost all the distilleries set up exhibits on the lawn, and merchants display and sell all kinds of bourbon-related items there, from books to foodstuffs. There are also demonstrations of barrel making, and the lawn is well within hearing range of the outdoor concerts taking place on a nearby stage. Not surprisingly, the Spirit Garden, where visitors can purchase bourbon drinks and beer, is one of the most popular sites. Venues for festival activities are scattered throughout Bardstown and may change from year to year, so be sure to double-check locations.

A Jim Beam barrel-racing team.

(Clockwise from top, left) The Buffalo Trace barrel-racing team. Buffalo Trace master distiller Harlen Wheatley. Gala guests mingle with Heaven Hill master distiller Parker Beam, and one attendee shows off a Four Roses tattoo. Jim Beam master distiller Fred Noe and a gala attendee compare footwear.

Distillery employees practice throughout the year to compete in the Saturday morning World Championship Bourbon Barrel Relay. Men's, women's, and mixed teams, as well as individuals, participate in the competition, which is based on the skills required to properly store barrels in a warehouse. The teams roll water-filled barrels around a course, and each barrel has to finish bung side up. A combination of the best time and the proper bung orientation wins the competition.

The festival is a good time to meet many of the people involved in the bourbon industry. All the master distillers are on hand for many of

Bardstown

the events, and they will certainly be in attendance at Saturday night's Great Kentucky Bourbon Tasting and Gala.

For details about tickets and events, call 800-638-4877. The Bourbon Festival staff will be glad to mail you a brochure. You can also buy tickets online at http://www.kybourbonfestival.com/.

Where to Eat and Drink

Most of the best food in Bardstown can be found in restaurants serving traditional southern cuisine. Pricing is indicated as follows: $—inexpensive, with most entrees priced at $15 or less; $$—moderate, at $16 to $25; and $$$—expensive, at $26 or higher. Reservations are recommended, especially during the Bourbon Festival.

BJ's Steakhouse—201 Camptown Road, 502-348-5070, http://www.bjssteakhouse.com. American, steaks, $$.

Circa Restaurant—103 East Stephen Foster Avenue, 502-348-5409, http://www.restaurant-circa.com/. Fine dining, $$–$$$.

Kentucky Bourbon House—107 East Stephen Foster Avenue, 502-507-8338, http://www.kentuckybourbonhouse.com/. Southern, $$. Bourbon tastings daily from 4 to 10 p.m.

Kurtz Restaurant—418 East Stephen Foster Avenue, 502-348-8964, http://www.bardstownparkview.com/dining.htm. Southern, $$.

My Old Kentucky Dinner Train—602 North Third Street, 502-348-7300 or 866-801-3463, http://www.kydinnertrain.com. American, $$.

Kentucky Bourbon Festival auction.

The historic Old Talbott Tavern has both a restaurant and lodging.

Old Talbott Tavern—107 West Stephen Foster Avenue, 502-348-3494 or 800-482-8376, http://www.talbotts.com. American, plus a good bourbon bar, $–$$.

The Rickhouse Restaurant & Lounge—Xavier Drive, 502-348-2832, http://www.therickhouse-bardstown.com/. American, steaks, $$–$$$.

Rosemark Haven Restaurant & Wine Bar—714 North Third Street, 502-348-8218, http://www.rosemarkhaven.com/dinners.html. American, $$–$$$.

Where to Stay

Hotel space is very limited during the Bourbon Festival. Even though Bardstown has many bed-and-breakfasts, most have only a few rooms. Keep in mind that you could stay in Louisville, which isn't far from Bardstown. Rates listed are the establishment's lowest. Special features and suites cost more, and daily rates can vary, so you will probably be quoted a higher rate, depending on when you want to stay.

Bardstown Parkview Motel—418 East Stephen Foster Avenue, 502-348-5983 or 800-732-2384, http://www.bardstownparkview.com/. $70.

Beautiful Dreamer Bed & Breakfast—440 East Stephen Foster Avenue, 502-348-4004 or 800-811-8312, http://bdreamerbb.com/. $149.

Best Western General Nelson Inn—411 West Stephen Foster Avenue, 502-348-3977 or 800-225-3977, http:// www.generalnelson.com. $68. This is the venue for several Bourbon Festival events.

Bardstown

Hill House, in the town of Loretto, is near Maker's Mark.

Hill House—110 Holy Cross Road, Loretto, 877-280-2300, http://www.thehillhouseky.com/. $95.

Jailer's Inn—111 West Stephen Foster Avenue, 502-348-5551 or 800-948-555, http://www.jailersinn.com/. $100.

Old Kentucky Home Stables and Bed & Breakfast—115 Samuels Road, Cox's Creek, 502-349-0408, http://www.farmstayus.com/farm/Kentucky/Old_Kentucky_Home_Stables. $115.

Old Talbott Tavern—107 West Stephen Foster Avenue, 502-348-3494 or 800-482-8376, http://www.talbotts.com. $65.

Rosemark Haven–714 North Third Street, 502-348-8218, http://www.rosemarkhaven.com/. $109.

Warehouse H at Barton 1792 Distillery.

Barton 1792 Distillery

300 Barton Road
Bardstown, KY 40004
502-331-4879 or 866-239-4690
http://www.1792bourbon.com

Hours: Monday–Friday, 9 a.m.–3 p.m.; Saturday, 10 a.m.–2 p.m. Tours are given year-round and start on the hour. Closed Sundays and major holidays. Call for information about special tours offered at other times.

Bourbons: 1792 Ridgemont Reserve, Colonel Lee, Kentucky Gentleman, Kentucky Tavern, Ten High, Tom Moore, Very Old Barton (80, 86, 90, and 100 proof)

Chief Executive: Mark Brown

Master Distiller: Ken Pierce, but his official title is director of distillation and quality assurance

Owner/Parent Company: Sazerac Company

Tours: The free tours take about two hours and end with a tasting of 1792 Ridgemont Reserve. Be aware that parts of the tour involve

Bardstown

steps, including 33 from the floor (often wet) of the still house to the still safe and you should *not* wear open-toed shoes.

What's Special:

- When the mash is cooking, it gives downtown Bardstown a distinctly aromatic atmosphere.
- The 192-acre property has twenty-eight aging warehouses.
- Water from an on-site spring is still used to make the bourbon here.
- One feature of the site is a fifteen-foot-tall, 8,000-gallon bourbon barrel that was a local high school's shop project (only in Kentucky).
- Many other brands of liquor owned by Sazerac are bottled on the premises.
- This was the first distillery to offer public tours, starting in 1957.
- Bardstown's Oscar Getz Museum of Whiskey History was originally housed here.
- The distillery's column still is six feet in diameter and fifty-five feet high.

History

Having a reliable source of limestone water is crucial for bourbon making, which is why so many Kentucky distilleries are located on rivers and streams. The Barton 1792 Distillery makes use of a third option: it has its own "never fail" spring.

The first distillery on the Morton's Spring site was owned by Willett & Franke, one of whose proprietors was John D. Willett (yes, there is still a Willett bourbon made today; see page 166). Willett's daughters married Thomas S. Moore and Benjamin F. Mattingly, and in 1876 their father-in-law transferred the distillery to the pair. Mattingly & Moore Distillery released Tom Moore bourbon in 1879, but the business was sold to investors in 1881. Mattingly left the company, but Moore stayed until he bought the property next to the Morton's Spring site and built his own distillery. Apparently, the investors who had purchased Mattingly & Moore were not very good businessmen, and they went bankrupt in 1916. Moore bought the property and merged it with his own operation, resulting in today's 192-acre site. But four years later came Prohibition.

The Moore family managed to keep the property and reopened the distillery after repeal but then sold it to Harry Teur, who renamed it Barton and modernized the facility. No one seems to know how he came up with the name, but according to one story, he picked it out of a hat. Barton was subsequently sold to Oscar Getz and Lester Abelson (coincidentally, another pair of brothers-in-law). After Barton filled its one millionth barrel in 1957, Getz, who was keenly interested in bourbon history, opened a museum on the grounds and invited the public to take

A plaque dedicated to Thomas Moore.

tours, beginning an industry practice that is common today. Eventually, the collection was moved to Spalding Hall and became the Oscar Getz Museum of Whiskey History.

Barton was a major player in the consolidation of bourbon brands that occurred in the 1970s and 1980s. Barton itself was bought in 1993 by the company that would become Constellation Brands. In a nod to history, Constellation renamed the distillery Tom Moore in 2008, but it turned out to be a very short-lived moniker. Sazerac (also the parent company of Buffalo Trace Distillery) acquired Tom Moore in 2009 and changed the name to Barton 1792 to include a reference to the company's premium bourbon—1792 Ridgemont Reserve, which had been released in 2003 (1792 is the year Kentucky became a state).

The Tour

The facility at Barton 1792 has an authentically industrial feel. Most of the larger distilling buildings date from the 1940s and were built for function, not aesthetics. Trucks rumble in and out of the grounds past the Visitors Center, and glass and machinery rattle loudly in the bottling plant. It's like traveling back in time to mid-twentieth-century America, when manufacturing drove the economy.

The combination gift shop and tasting room, where tours begin, is located in the remodeled building that originally housed Oscar Getz's collection of bourbon memorabilia. Your tour guide will cover the history and details of bourbon, including a description of the aging process, on a visit to one of the warehouses. A full fifty-three-gallon barrel weighs about 520 pounds, but the whiskey begins to evaporate almost immediately. The first year, about 10 percent is lost, with another 3 or 4 percent lost each year thereafter. This is why bourbons aged more than a decade start to get pricey: there are simply fewer bottles per barrel.

Bourbon warehouses are constructed using an interlocking system of beams, resembling giant Tinker Toys, to allow air circulation. If one side of the warehouse becomes too heavy, with too many new, full barrels in one place and too many older and evaporating barrels in another, the whole structure could go out of balance and collapse. So you'll notice plumb lines strategically placed in Warehouse H; these are used to measure any structural shifts and ensure that the 10 million pounds of bourbon stored there stays put.

The second stop on the tour is the still house for a look at Barton's impressive distilling apparatus. The five-story-high column still is six and a half feet wide and can distill more than 100 gallons an hour. (At this point, the guide might mention that as of 2011, the human population of Kentucky was 4.4 million, whereas the number of aging bourbon barrels in warehouses throughout the state was 4.7 million.) After gazing up at the still, you'll climb three flights of metal stairs to the room housing the gleaming copper spirit safe, where there will be plenty of time to have your photo snapped.

The Barton 1792 women's barrel-racing team on the distillery's practice course.

Distiller Ken Pierce nosing new whiskey from the spirit safe.

Barton's bottling operation is impressively efficient. There are six bot-tling lines, and each can be changed in about twelve minutes to accom-modate different products. In addition to its own bourbons, Barton does a lot of contract bottling for other distillers, including California brandy distillers. Parent company Sazerac owns several brands of vodkas and

Adding stoppers to bottles of 1792 Ridgemont Reserve.

gins, which you may also see being bottled. The plant is noisy—a cross between a roller coaster and a light rail system, accented with the high-pitched click of glass on metal. (It's quieter when the bottles on the line are plastic.)

Like all good distillery tours, this one ends with a tasting. Little snifters of 1792 Ridgemont Reserve are a nice touch. Trays of bourbon balls are offered too, and no one minds if you have more than one.

The Bourbon

When current director of distillation Ken Pierce joined Barton's in 1994, he was given the task of creating a premium small-batch bourbon. The result, released in 2003, was 1792 Ridgemont Reserve (the bourbon you will sample at the end of the tour). The name honors the year of Kentucky's statehood and the name of the still in which the bourbon is produced. (Apparently, some stills, like some automobiles, are given names.)

Barton does not release the exact proportions used in its mash bills, but it has disclosed that 1792 Ridgemont Reserve has a higher rye content than most bourbons. This is evident from the first whiff of the whiskey. The nose is all about spice. Joining the expected vanilla and caramel are notes of coffee and chocolate. If there is any fruit at all, it is apple, but you really have to concentrate to taste it. The bourbon is bottled at 93.7 proof, so the longer it sits in the glass, the more layers of flavor are revealed. The finish is long and spicy.

Visitors pose with Barton 1792's fifteen-foot-tall bourbon barrel.

The signature brand of the distillery is the six-year-old Very Old Barton. When it was first made in the 1940s, it was aged two years longer than most other bourbons—hence the name. Long the best-selling bourbon in Kentucky, it is bottled at 80, 86, 90, and 100 proof. The distillery gift shop sells the 86-proof Very Old Barton in addition to 1792 Ridgemont Reserve. The 100-proof version is bottled in bond and well worth seeking out at a local liquor store.

Travel Advice

Barton 1792 is less than a five-minute drive from the Bardstown Courthouse Square. Go west on Stephen Foster Avenue for a quarter mile and turn left onto Barton Road. The distillery is half a mile farther on your right.

Nearby Attractions

All the attractions of Bardstown are within a few minutes of one another, but you will certainly want to visit the **Oscar Getz Museum of Whiskey History** (114 North Fifth Street, 502-348-2999, http://www .whiskeymuseum.com). Originally housed at Barton, it is now located at Spalding Hill, just a short drive across Stephen Foster Avenue from the distillery, tucked behind St. Joseph's Proto-Cathedral. The collection of bourbon-related artifacts spans more than two centuries and includes antique distilling equipment, rare bottles and other containers, glassware, advertisements, and prescriptions for bourbon written during Prohibition. As a bourbon lover, you'll probably want to avert your eyes from Carrie Nation's hatchet, which is displayed in a little case next to a photograph of the temperance zealot.

Heaven Hill Bourbon Heritage Center

> 1311 Gilkey Run Road
> Bardstown, KY 40004
> 502-337-1000
> http://www.bourbonheritagecenter.com

Hours: Monday–Saturday, 10 a.m.–5 p.m.; Sunday, noon–4 p.m. Tours are given year-round. Closed major holidays.

Bourbons: Evan Williams, Evan Williams Single Barrel Vintage, Elijah Craig Single Barrel 12-Year-Old, Elijah Craig Single Barrel 18-Year-Old, Larceny, Parker's Heritage Collection (very limited release), Heaven Hill, Henry McKenna, Henry McKenna Single Barrel, Fighting Cock, Old Fitzgerald, Old Fitzgerald's 1849, Old Fitzgerald Very

The 1792 Ridgemont Reserve bottling line.

Heaven Hill Bourbon Heritage Center.

Special 12-Year-Old, Cabin Still, J. W. Dant, Echo Spring, Mattingly & Moore, J. T. S. Brown, T. W. Samuels, Kentucky Deluxe, Kentucky Supreme

Ryes: Rittenhouse Straight Rye, Pikesville Straight Rye

Other Liquors: Bernheim Original Kentucky Straight Wheat Whiskey, Evan Williams Honey Reserve (liqueur made with bourbon), Corn and Rye New Make Whiskeys, Mellow Corn Kentucky Straight Corn Whiskey, and a large catalog of vodkas (plain and flavored), rums, tequilas, gins, and other spirits

Chief Executive: Max L. Shapira

Master Distillers: Parker Beam and Craig Beam

Owner/Parent Company: Heaven Hill Distilleries Inc.

Tours: The Mini Tour, which lasts about half an hour, is free and is offered many times throughout the day. The Deluxe Tour, also free and offered throughout the day, lasts an hour and a half. The Behind the Scenes Tour is three hours and costs $25. A half-hour Trolley Tour of Bardstown is $5. Reservations for the last two tours can be made online or by calling the Bourbon Heritage Center.

What's Special:
- Heaven Hill opened in 1935—after the repeal of Prohibition.
- It is the largest family-owned and -operated independent (not publicly traded) producer and marketer of distilled spirits in the United States.
- Heaven Hill owns the second-largest amount of aging bourbon in the world, with an inventory of more than 900,000 barrels.

Bardstown

- After a 1996 fire destroyed its Bardstown distillery, Heaven Hill bought the Bernheim Distillery in Louisville in 1999, where all the company's bourbon is made today.
- The Bourbon Heritage Center, which opened in 2004, has won numerous awards, including *Whisky Magazine*'s Icon and Visitor Attraction of the Year.
- You can join the distillery's Bardstown Whiskey Society (www .bardstownwhiskeysociety.com) and receive notice of special events and its monthly e-newsletter the *Barrelhouse Chronicle*.
- Heaven Hill plans to open an Evan Williams microdistillery and a history exhibit on Louisville's Whiskey Row in the fall of 2013, just a couple of blocks south of the probable location of Evan Williams's eighteenth-century distillery.

History

In addition to bringing relief to bourbon drinkers, the end of Prohibition on December 5, 1933, created business opportunities for entrepreneurs who had managed to retain some capital even in the midst of the Great Depression. Before 1920 there had been more than 200 operating distilleries in Kentucky. Only about one-third of them reopened in 1934 to make bourbon for thirsty Americans.

With the number of distilleries seriously diminished, brothers David, Ed, Gary, George, and Mose Shapira recognized that starting a new distillery could be a profitable venture. The Shapiras bought property south of Bardstown where one William Heavenhill had had farm in the nineteenth century. They split the farmer's name in two and christened their new distillery Heaven Hill.

Even today, one obstacle to opening a new distillery is how long you have to wait for a salable product. Although it doesn't take long to make whiskey, you can't sell it until it has aged for several years. The Shapiras got their brand into the marketplace quickly by selling their new whiskey when it was just two years old, the age at which it could legally be called "straight bourbon." Bourbon Falls Kentucky Straight Bourbon made enough money to keep the business going until the brothers could release bourbon that had been aged longer. That bourbon was four-year-old Heaven Hill.

In 1946 the Shapiras recognized that although they knew how to build a business, they really didn't know much about bourbon, other than what they were learning on the job. (There's a big difference between owning a baseball team and being able to hit home runs.) So they hired a member of the Beam family, distiller Henry Homel. Beams have been at the helm of Heaven Hill's distilling ever since. In 1948 Homel's

The filling room, part of the Behind the Scenes Tour.

Visitors read about the history of Heaven Hill in the Bourbon Heritage Center.

Custom-designed machinery in the bottling plant.

cousin, Earl Beam, left the Jim Beam Distillery to become Heaven Hill's master distiller. Earl's son, Parker Beam, started working at Heaven Hill in 1960 and eventually became master distiller himself, a position he still holds, although most of the daily distillery operation is now in the hands of *his* son, Craig Beam. Meanwhile, the Shapira family is still in charge of the business, with the children and grandchildren of the original brothers continuing to expand the company's presence both in America and abroad.

This growth is all the more impressive in light of the catastrophe that occurred at Heaven Hill on the stormy afternoon of November 7, 1996. At around two o'clock, a fire started in one of the warehouses (it might have been sparked by lightning, but no cause has ever been determined). Warehouse interiors are made of wood, designed to allow maximum air circulation, and they are filled with alcohol-soaked wooden barrels that act like resin-soaked kindling in a woodstove. It is impossible to stop a bourbon-fueled fire once it has started. The best possible outcome is containment—preventing the fire from leaping to other buildings. But in this case, that too proved to be almost impossible.

The storm front was accompanied by winds of forty to fifty miles per hour, which caused the fire to spread rapidly. Soon half a dozen other warehouses had caught fire. Flames shot hundreds of feet in the air, and the light and heat of the fire were accompanied by the percussive cracks of thousands of exploding bourbon barrels. A dozen engine companies, including two from as far away as Louisville, responded to the scene, but all the firefighters could do was pump water onto the buildings that had not yet caught. Worst of all, by four o'clock the distillery itself, located downhill from the warehouses, was engulfed. Footage shot from news helicopters showed streams of flaming whiskey flowing from the burning warehouses to the distillery buildings.

Remarkably, no one was seriously injured, but almost 8 million gallons of bourbon were destroyed. (This was estimated to represent 2 percent of the world's bourbon supply at the time.) The good news was that Heaven Hill's proprietary yeast strain dating from 1935 had been rescued.

Barton, Jim Beam, and Brown-Forman allowed Heaven Hill to distill in their plants until 1999, when the company purchased the Bernheim Distillery in Louisville from Diageo. Heaven Hill continues to make bourbon there today. It also enlarged its bottling operation in Bardstown and rebuilt its warehouses. And in 2004 the Bourbon Heritage Center opened to visitors.

Bardstown

The Tours

Even though Heaven Hill no longer has a working distillery in Bardstown, visitors to the Bourbon Heritage Center can still get an excellent sense of what is involved in the bourbon-making process. The center's design was inspired by traditional warehouse architecture, and it is chock full of informative, interactive exhibits on the history of bourbon and its place in Kentucky history. Each of the Heritage Center's site-based tours begins in the Evan Williams Theater, where a short film, *Portrait of Heaven Hill,* contains narrative about the suitability of Kentucky's climate and natural resources for bourbon making. Fittingly (given that two of Heaven Hill's signature bourbons are named after them), bourbon pioneers Elijah Craig and Evan Williams make onscreen appearances. Each of the tours ends with a tasting in the Barrel Bar inside the Parker Beam Tasting Barrel, where bourbons are served in Glencairn glasses placed on built-in bar-top lights to show off the whiskies' colors.

After a tasting, you can take your time exploring the gift shop, which surrounds the Tasting Barrel. Several interactive exhibits about bourbon flavors are interspersed with the displays of merchandise, which includes a large array of books, signature glassware, clothing, and gourmet food items made with Heaven Hill products. A small number of bottles of Parker Beam's very limited edition Heritage Collection are also available in the gift shop. A different bottling is released each year.

Mini Tour

If you are planning to visit more than one distillery in a day or happen to be in Bardstown for the Bourbon Festival, the thirty-minute Mini Tour is a fine introduction to Heaven Hill. After the orientation film, your guide will take you around the exhibits in the Bourbon Heritage Center, which is filled with historic photos, distilling paraphernalia, and time lines. Although these exhibits are very detailed and self-explanatory, the guide will field questions and, of course, lead you in the tasting of Evan Williams Single Barrel Vintage in the Barrel Bar. Visitors are given vials of scents to sniff in order to warm up their nosing "muscles." Small pitchers of water are also provided so you can experiment with how a splash of water affects the whiskey's flavors. There is no charge for the tour.

Deluxe Tour

The Deluxe Tour is also free. From the theater, the guide leads visitors outside to Warehouse Y for a detailed explanation of the aging process, with an emphasis on the influence of the barrel char, the barrel's position in the warehouse, and the number of years to maturity. Then he

A post-tour tasting in the Parker Beam Tasting Barrel.

or she will take you back to the Barrel Bar to taste two bourbons—Evan Williams Single Barrel Vintage and Elijah Craig 12-Year-Old—allowing you to compare and contrast.

Behind the Scenes Tour

Heaven Hill makes a lot of bourbon, but it accounts for only about a quarter of the company's sales. It also owns dozens of brands of spirits and imports and distributes many more. Most of this liquor winds up at the massive production plant next door to the Bourbon Heritage Center, in which about a million cases are bottled each year. This is the focus of the Behind the Scenes Tour.

The Shapiras have invested in custom-built, state-of-the-art technology to handle the enormous volume of product passing through the facility. After the same orientation film shown for the other tours, a van will whisk you to the barrel-filling building, where a series of conveyors rolls the barrels into position. This saves the backs of the staff; all they have to do is run the computerized filling machinery. A display of barrel heads on the wall by the entrance marks the important Heaven Hill barrel milestones. The first barrel was filled with whiskey in 1935, and

Bardstown

it took twenty-six years to reach the millionth barrel. It's a measure of Heaven Hill's (and the bourbon industry's) growth that the gap between the five millionth and six millionth barrels (the latter filled in 2010) was only four years.

The gleaming bottling operation is mesmerizing, like an over-twenty-one version of Willie Wonka's Chocolate Factory. Thousands of bottles of various shapes and sizes zip along steel channels, where they are filled, labeled, sealed, boxed, and stacked. Helical conveyor towers carrying cardboard cases look like escaped carnival rides. There's even a machine that squirts glue on the box flaps before closing and sealing them and a giant plastic shrink-wrapping machine to wrap flats stacked high with cardboard cases.

The tour includes a warehouse visit before concluding with a tasting of any two of three bourbons—Evan Williams Single Barrel Vintage, Elijah Craig 12-Year-Old, and Elijah Craig 18-Year-Old. The Behind the Scenes Tour is limited to six participants at a time, lasts about three hours, and costs $25 per person. Reservations must be made in advance.

Trolley Tour

The half-hour Trolley Tour leaves from the Bourbon Heritage Center and offers a good introduction to the history and sights of Bardstown. The route may vary, depending on the time of day and the interests of the passengers, but among the popular sites are My Old Kentucky Home State Park, Old Bardstown Village, Old Talbott Tavern, My Old Kentucky Dinner Train, and the Wickland mansion. The tour costs $5 per person, and reservations are required.

The Bourbon

Heaven Hill produces more than twenty bourbons and offers three of its best at the tour-end tastings. A bottling of Evan Williams Single Barrel Vintage has been released each year since 1995. Craig and Parker Beam select individual barrels that have the profile they want, and the bourbon is bottled from each barrel without mingling. This means that each vintage is a little different, even though the proof is always 86.6 and the age is about nine years. (The statement "Put in the Oak," followed by the year, appears on each bottle.) The little lights on the Barrel Bar bring out the bourbon's bright gold sparkle. The nose features caramel and oak. Wood persists on the palate, dominating the orange notes; spice and wood dominate the finish.

At 94 proof, the Elijah Craig 12-Year-Old immediately gets your attention with a big vanilla nose. The fruit on the palate takes second place to spice, including cinnamon and nutmeg, and the coppery-colored

Barrel number 5,500,000.

bourbon finishes with more sweetness than it begins with. It's a small-batch bourbon that has been mingled from several barrels.

Given its age, it is not surprising that the Elijah Craig 18-Year-Old has a darker amber color than the other two bourbons. Both the nose and the palate are a lovely balance of vanilla and nutty caramel. This single-barrel bourbon has a lightly spicy finish that lingers luxuriously.

Travel Advice

From Bardstown's Courthouse Square, take US 150 (East Stephen Foster Avenue) for eight-tenths of a mile past My Old Kentucky Home State Park and turn right onto Parkway Drive (KY 49). After about a mile, you will come to a fork in the road, where you'll see the Heaven Hill warehouses. Bear to the right, and the Bourbon Heritage Center is on your right. The drive from the center of Bardstown takes about five minutes.

Kentucky Bourbon Distillers and Willett Distillery

1869 Loretto Road
Bardstown, KY 40004
502-348-0081
http://www.kentuckybourbonwhiskey.com

Hours: Tours are given year-round, Monday–Saturday, at 10 a.m. and 2 p.m. The tasting room is open Monday–Friday, 9 a.m.– 5 p.m., and Saturday, 10 a.m.– 3 p.m. Closed major holidays.

Bourbons: Willett Pot Still Reserve, Noah's Mill, Rowan's Creek, Pure Kentucky XO, Kentucky Vintage, Johnny Drum Kentucky Straight Bourbon Whiskey, Johnny Drum Private Stock, Old Bardstown Black Label, Old Bardstown Estate Bottled, Old Bardstown Gold Label, limited-edition 17-Year-Old Vintage Bourbon

Chief Executive: Even Kulsveen

Master Distiller: Drew Kulsveen

Owner/Parent Company: Kentucky Bourbon Distillers Ltd.

Tours: Tour of the working distillery includes the still house, a warehouse, and the gift shop/tasting room. Tours include a taste of any two Kentucky Bourbon Distillers' bourbons, except for the very expensive, limited-production Willett Pot Still Reserve.

What's Special:
• This is a small, independent, family-owned distillery.

A bull made out of barrels (the signs read, "No bull, just bourbon").

Kentucky Bourbon Distillers and Willett Distillery.

- The distillery has both a pot still and a column still, which can be used independently or in combination.
- Until 2012, the bourbons from Kentucky Bourbon Distillers (KBD) were bottled from existing stocks of aging barrels bought from distilleries that had gone out of business, such as Stitzel-Weller, or bought from working distilleries and aged at the KBD site.
- The distillery, including its eight bonded warehouses, is situated on a hill overlooking Heaven Hill.
- Development of the distillery property is ongoing, including the construction of two buildings to accommodate overnight guests. The bed-and-breakfast is scheduled to open in 2014.

History

Many bourbon travelers combine a morning visit to the Heaven Hill Bourbon Heritage Center with an afternoon jaunt to Maker's Mark, which is about half an hour away via Loretto Road. But just a minute's drive from the Heritage Center, a few hundred yards past the ruins of Heaven Hill's original distillery, you'll find the very antithesis of a million-case-a-year operation.

Bardstown

The Willett Distilling Company was founded by several members of one family in 1935. Lambert Willett bought the property, and his sons A. L. "Thompson" Willett and Johnny Willett built the distillery. Willett's best-known brand was Old Bardstown, and it remained small by the standards of its neighbor. By the 1970s, the company was producing about fifty barrels a day and had eight warehouses. With the downturn in the bourbon market, the plant was converted to making fuel alcohol. Unfortunately, the end of the 1970s oil crisis shrank the demand for industrial ethanol too, and Willett's closed in the early 1980s. But this is not another sad story of a closed and abandoned distillery.

Thompson Willett's daughter Martha married a Norwegian named Even Kulsveen, who purchased the property in 1984 and founded Kentucky Bourbon Distillers Ltd. Kulsveen, along with his son Drew, daughter Britt, and son-in-law Hunter Chavanne, have run KBD as a successful bottler of bourbons made under contract by other (undisclosed) distillers. Willett Pot Still Reserve was introduced in 2008; it's an award-winning single-barrel bourbon aged eight to ten years and bottled at 47 proof. But that's still not the end of the story.

For three decades, Even Kulsveen and his family have slowly been restoring and refurbishing the Willett Distillery. New, custom-made distilling equipment was commissioned from Vendome Copper & Brass Works, which complements some of the equipment that remains from the distillery's founding in 1935. And as of January 2012, bourbon is once again being produced at the Willett Distilling Company. A 103-proof bourbon was put into barrels on Thompson Willett's 103rd birthday, signaling the rebirth of Willett Distillery.

The Tour

Unless you are part of a group that has made special arrangements, tours at the big distilleries are usually led by staff guides, not by the master distiller. But Willett is a small operation, and chances are good (at least until production increases considerably) that your tour guide will be master distiller Drew Kulsveen. His pride in his family's distilling history and the pleasure he takes in explaining the features of the current plant make this a true insiders' tour.

Visitors meet in the gift shop/tasting room. It's a short walk to the still house, which has been restored and enhanced with carefully selected materials ranging from limestone and brick to custom-made ironwork. You'll climb a wide flight of stairs to the floor containing the tops of the fermentation tanks. This overlooks the room that houses Willett's new copper pot still. In summer, the fermentation room is cooled with

*Master dis-
tiller Drew
Kulsveen.*

*Willett's
copper pot
still.*

Red door at Willett Distillery.

Sour Mash Bourbon Whiskey barrel.

a series of large, handsome, belt-driven ceiling fans powered by a small enclosed motor, which prevents dangerous sparks.

When the tour returns to the main floor, Kulsveen will fill a glass with new whiskey from the spirit safe and pass it around for visitors to nose. The tour then moves to the barrel-filling house, before going to one of the warehouses. The hilltop elevation (more than 640 feet above sea level, higher than any other warehouse in Nelson County) allows a striking amount of air to circulate between the barrels. You seldom encounter this much breeze in a bourbon warehouse.

The tour ends in the gift shop and tasting room, housed in the building that originally served as the distillery offices.

The Bourbons

Several KBD brands are offered for tasting, but in accordance with state law, each visitor is limited to two small tastes, so you'll have to make some choices. Here's a rundown of a few of the KBD brands offered:

- Johnny Drum Private Stock (101 proof)—caramel nose and taste dominated by oak and showing some hints of ginger
- Kentucky Vintage (90 proof)—light caramel character supplemented by notes of tobacco and leather
- Noah's Mill (114.3 proof)—oaky and spicy; tame its heat with a splash of water
- Old Bardstown Gold Label (80 proof)—dominated by corn and vanilla, with more fruit than many KBD bourbons
- Pure Kentucky XO (107 proof)— complex fruit, which can be better appreciated with the addition of a little water
- Rowan's Creek (101 proof)—vanilla, dark fruits, and more than a hint of nuttiness

Maker's Mark

3350 Burks Spring Road
Loretto, KY 40037
270-865-2881
http://www.makersmark.com

Hours: Monday–Saturday, 10 a.m.–4:30 p.m.; Sunday, 1–4:30 p.m.
Closed major holidays and Sundays in January and February.
Bourbons: Maker's Mark, Maker's 46
Chief Executive: Rob Samuels
Master Distiller: Greg Davis
Owner/Parent Company: Beam Inc.

Maker's Mark.

Tour: The tour-end tasting includes bourbon balls and samples of both
  whiskies.

What's Special:

• Maker's Mark was designated a National Historic Landmark in 1980.

• You can dip your own bottle of bourbon in the signature red wax.

• If you join Maker's Mark Ambassadors, your name will be put on a
  barrel in the warehouse.

• Nighttime tours with holiday lights and music are given in December.

• The site is also an arboretum, and many trees have identification signs.

History

With its distinctive red wax–covered bottle neck, Maker's Mark is in-
stantly recognizable at any restaurant bar or on any store shelf. The look
is a triumph of branding that dates from the middle of the twentieth
century, even though the Samuels family has been making bourbon for
eight generations, ever since Robert Samuels settled in Kentucky in the
1780s.

   In 1840 Robert Samuels's grandson, T. W., build the family's first commercial distillery near Samuels Depot in Nelson County. (Before then,

they had made whiskey mainly for consumption by the family and select friends.) Over the next three generations, until Prohibition closed the distillery in 1919, T. W. Samuels bourbon was made and sold. In 1933, at the end of Prohibition, T. W. Samuels reopened, but the distillery was sold in 1943. As it turned out, the family couldn't stay out of the whiskey business, and that's when Maker's Mark was born.

In 1952 Bill Samuels Sr. started experimenting with whiskey recipes by baking bread with different proportions of grains. T. W. Samuels bourbon had been made with corn, rye, and malted barley, but Samuels was looking for something a little different. He consulted with Julian "Pappy" Van Winkle of the Stitzel-Weller Distillery in Louisville, who suggested using wheat in place of rye, as the Van Winkle bourbons do. Samuels took this advice, and his experiments evolved into the mash bill used by Maker's Mark today—70 percent corn, 14 percent red winter wheat, and 16 percent malted barley. But he needed a distillery.

In 1953 Samuels bought the 200-acre Star Hill Farm in Marion County, near Loretto. Bourbon had been distilled on the site since 1805, and it contained a small distillery and several historic buildings, all in need of repair. Samuels not only repaired the buildings but also restored them to their period charm, painting the wooden buildings black with bright red trim and planting native Kentucky trees on the grounds. The restoration was done with such meticulous attention to detail that Maker's Mark Distillery was later designated a National Historic Landmark, the first distillery in the United States given that distinction.

So why is it called Maker's Mark? Credit for the name, and for much of what gives the bourbon its identity, goes to Samuels's wife, Marge, who was a collector of pewter and of antique cognac bottles. Pewter pieces are stamped with the distinctive marks of their makers, so Mrs. Samuels suggested that this distinctive, handmade bourbon should also bear its maker's mark. She got the idea for the red wax from a similar wax on cognac bottles. The circle on the wax seal and the paper label features a star (for Star Hill Farm), the letter S for Samuels, and roman numeral IV for the fourth generation of commercial distillers in the family. Every bottle is hand-dipped in red wax, and every label is hand-cut and pasted on each bottle.

In deference to his Scotch-Irish heritage, Samuels spelled whisky in the traditional rather than the American way on his label. Samuels prided himself on his handmade "small-batch" bourbon, which was sold almost exclusively in Kentucky for twenty years, from the time it was introduced to the market in 1959. That all changed in 1980.

By the 1970s, Bill Samuels Jr. was working for his father at the distillery. In 1980 the Wall Street Journal ran a front-page article about the picturesque distillery situated in a beautiful Kentucky valley. Maker's Mark suddenly became an international brand, and demand and sales soared. Samuels Jr. succeeded his father as company president in 1982. Displaying much of the same marketing savvy as his mother, he wrote copy for many of the first distinctive magazine and billboard ads for Maker's Mark. He was perfectly happy to don colorful costumes and appear in many of the ads himself, adding to Maker's reputation as a unique bourbon in a crowded field. The bourbon was so popular that capacity for distillation was doubled in 2002 by replicating the nineteenth-century distilling equipment.

In 2010 Bill Jr.'s son, Rob Samuels, was named chief operating officer of Maker's Mark and general manager of the distillery, now owned by Beam Inc. But even in "retirement," the colorful Bill Samuels Jr., now chairman emeritus, continues to be the public face of Maker's Mark.

The Tour

Today, visitors to Maker's Mark can watch the bottling process and even dip a bottle themselves. If you happen to visit the distillery during the winter holiday season, you'll find that the employees working on the bottling line appear to have been borrowed from a certain cookie maker that claims its products are made by elves in trees.

Elf togs notwithstanding, any season is a fine time to visit Maker's Mark. With its idyllic setting, charming historic buildings, and hospitable tour guides, the distillery is appealing not only to bourbon lovers but also to anyone interested in learning about Kentucky history and spending a few quiet hours in the country. Spring is spectacular, when many of the distillery's flowering trees are in bloom and make a striking contrast against the black-painted buildings.

Tours begin in the red frame distiller's house, which at one time was the Samuels family home. Bill Samuels Sr.'s office is preserved and lined with photo portraits of family members that "tell" their stories. (There's a touch of Hogwarts School of Witchcraft and Wizardry at work here.)

As you leave the distiller's house on the way to the still house, you'll see the firehouse, complete with a bright red antique fire engine—a reminder that fire is the number-one safety concern at every distillery. After you cross the road, you'll climb a short flight of limestone steps to enter the still house. Your guide will show off samples of the corn, wheat, and barley used to make the whiskey and explain the distilling process as the tour progresses from the cypress fermenting tanks to the gleaming copper column stills and doublers.

The bottling house is the next stop, and then into Warehouse D, where you'll learn that Maker's Mark is the only distillery that undertakes the laborious task of rotating its barrels through various levels of

Factory "elves" dip holiday bottles of bourbon in wax.

Spirit safes.

Bill Samuels Jr.

the warehouse to achieve a uniform aging flavor. You may also notice metal plates with names etched on them affixed to some of the barrels. These are the names of Maker's Mark Ambassadors—essentially, the bourbon's "fan club"—and these nameplates are one of the perks of membership. (For full details of the program, go to the Maker's Mark website.)

From the warehouse, your guide will lead you through a door into the very contemporary interior of the gift shop and tasting room. Provided you are at least twenty-one years old, you'll get to sample Maker's Mark, Maker's 46, and a Maker's Mark bourbon ball chocolate candy. You'll also have plenty of time to stock up on all the red-and-black signature Maker's Mark "swag," from barware and bourbon to clothing and golf gear.

Weather permitting, spend some time strolling the grounds, which can be as relaxing as sipping some Maker's Mark. The small Toll House Café, near the distillery entrance, serves sandwiches, salads, and desserts every day from 11:30 a.m. to 4:30 p.m. Group reservations can be made by calling 270-865-4982.

The Bourbon

The signature Maker's Mark bourbon in the square bottle with the red wax top is distilled at 120 proof, goes into the barrel at 110 proof (instead of the usual 125 proof), and is bottled at 90 proof. The mash bill is the same as it was back in the 1950s: 70 percent corn, 14 percent red winter wheat, and 16 percent malted barley. The yeast is cultured on-site and is a strain that has been in the Samuels family for five generations. Maker's Mark has a bright amber hue, and the high proportion of corn gives it a very sweet nose from which vanilla, caramel, and notes of orange emerge. It is medium bodied and smooth on the palate and has a soft, clean finish.

Unlike most other distilleries, which produce more than one brand of bourbon, Maker's Mark made only its original bourbon for many years. However, it created variation by issuing commemorative versions of its square, wax-topped bottle. Blue wax showed up to celebrate a University of Kentucky national basketball championship. Holiday bottles marked Halloween, Thanksgiving, and Christmas.

Finally, in 2010, the new Maker's 46 bourbon was introduced, with much fanfare. Maker's 46 is 94 proof, slightly higher than the original. It is made by dumping mature Maker's Mark from its barrel, lining the

Bottles are decorated for various holidays.

Tasting at the end of the tour.

The site is also an arboretum, and spring brings beautiful blooms to the trees.

barrel with ten additional charred oak staves, reintroducing the whiskey, and aging it for several more months. The name is derived from the number assigned to the charring process developed by Independent Staves (the barrel maker) owner Brad Boswell and former master distiller Kevin Smith to achieve just the right amount of char. The resulting bourbon is less sweet on the nose and a bit darker in color, and it shows more wood and spice than original Maker's Mark.

Travel Advice

Maker's Mark is located farther from a major highway than any of the other distilleries that offer tours, so more than a few would-be visitors have found themselves lost in the scenic Kentucky countryside in an effort to find it. This is especially true if you are heading to Maker's Mark on a dark December night for the "candlelight" tour (in reality, the candles are thousands of tiny fairy lights—no open flames in a distillery!). There are signs, but they are easy to miss.

From Bardstown, take East Stephen Foster Road just past My Old Kentucky Home State Park and turn right onto KY 49. This will take you past both Heaven Hill and Kentucky Bourbon Distillers along a wooded route. After about ten miles, staying straight puts you on KY 527. Follow this road for about four and a half miles to Burk Spring Road, and then follow the signs to Maker's Mark, about half a mile farther along.

Maker's Mark is half an hour south of Bardstown, and it takes about forty-five minutes to get to Bardstown from Louisville via I-65 or US 31E, or about an hour to get there from Lexington via the Bluegrass Parkway.

Nearby Attractions

Kentucky Cooperage (712 East Main Street, Lebanon, 270-692-4518, http://www.independentstavecompany.com), which makes barrels for all the bourbon distilleries except those owned by Brown-Forman, is less than twenty minutes east of Maker's Mark.

Limestone Branch Distillery (1280 Veterans Memorial Parkway, Lebanon, 270-699-9004, http://www.limestonebranch.com) is a small operation run by Beam descendants. They are currently selling a new, unaged whiskey (they actually call it "moonshine"). Tours are offered.

Lincoln's birthplace and boyhood home at Knob Creek are enshrined at the **Abraham Lincoln Birthplace National Historical Park** (2995 Lincoln Farm Road, Hodgenville, 270-358-3137, http://www.nps.gov/abli/index.htm), about a forty-five-minute drive from Maker's Mark.

The **Lincoln Homestead State Park** (5079 Lincoln Park Road, Springfield, 859-336-7461, http://www.parks.ky.gov/findparks/recparks/lh),

Barrels display the Limestone Branch name.

Limestone Branch Distillery.

his parents' courtship site, is about fifteen minutes north of Kentucky Cooperage.

The **Abbey of Gethsemani** (3642 Monks Road, Trappist, 270-699-9004, www.monks.org), once home to philosopher Thomas Merton and known for the bourbon fruitcake and candies made by the Trappist monks, is about twenty minutes west of the distillery.

Jim Beam Distillery

> 149 Happy Hollow Road
> Clermont, KY 40110
> 502-543-9877
> http://www.jimbeam.com

Hours: Monday–Saturday, 9 a.m.–4:30 p.m.; Sunday, 12–4:30 p.m. Closed major holidays and Sundays in January and February.

Bourbons: Jim Beam White Label, Jim Beam Black Label, Jim Beam Choice, Devil's Cut, Baker's, Basil Hayden, Booker's, Knob Creek, Old Crow, Old Grand-Dad (86, 100, and 114 proof), Old Taylor

Ryes: Jim Beam Rye, Knob Creek Rye, Old Overholt Rye

Other Liquors: Red Stag (cherry-infused bourbon), Red Stag Honey Tea, Red Stag Spiced

Chief Executive: Matthew Shattock
Master Distiller: Fred Noe
Owner/Parent Company: Beam Global
Tours: Tours of the Clermont distillery and the American Stillhouse, with interactive exhibits, were added in 2012. There is an $8 admission fee.
What's Special:
- Jim Beam White Label is the best-selling brand of bourbon worldwide.
- Current master distiller Fred Noe is the great-great-great-great-grandson of Jacob Beam (who was distilling in Kentucky in the 1790s) and the great-grandson of the distillery's namesake, Colonel James Beam.
- Beam has a second distillery in nearby Boston, Kentucky, and bottling facilities in Frankfort.
- Beam started bottling bourbon in what has become a series of collectible decanters in the early 1950s.
- Booker's, the first barrel-proof, unfiltered bourbon available to the consumer market, was released in 1988.
- The Clermont location includes a 34,000-square-foot research and development facility.
- Members of the Beam family have had a hand in making at least sixty different brands of bourbon from several distilleries.

History

There is probably no more widely recognized name in the bourbon industry than Jim Beam, and not just because it is the best-selling bourbon brand in the world. Beam family members have been distillers in Kentucky for seven generations; these whiskey makers can all trace their roots to an eighteenth-century Pennsylvanian of German descent named Johannes Jacob Boehm.

By the time Boehm arrived in central Kentucky in the 1780s, he had Anglicized his name to "Beam." He set up business as both a distiller and a miller near Blincoe (now Manton), about ten miles southeast of Bardstown. (Obviously, his occupations were connected, since milled grain could be made into whiskey.) One of Beam's sons, David, acted as his assistant, and they were selling whiskey by 1795.

David, who continued the business after his father's death in 1834, had two sons who also became distillers—David M. and John H. The latter founded Early Times Distillery nearby. John Beam named his bourbon to reflect his devotion to the traditional way of making whiskey in the "early times." The Early Times Distillery continued to make bourbon throughout the nineteenth century and into the twentieth, changing owners more than once before being closed by Prohibition. It was during

Jim Beam American Stillhouse Visitors Center and Gift Shop.

Prohibition that Brown-Forman, which needed additional stock to meet the demand for "medicinal" whiskey, bought the warehoused Early Times along with the brand name. Brown-Forman continues to make the brand at its Early Times Distillery in Louisville.

Meanwhile, David M. built a new distillery in about 1860, located northwest of Bardstown near the convent of the Sisters of Charity of Nazareth. (If you are driving south on US 31E into Bardstown, you'll see the twin towers of the church on your right. Warehouses on the former distillery property are now owned and used by Heaven Hill.) David M.'s son, James Beauregard Beam (yes, we've finally come to Jim Beam) and his brother-in-law, Albert Hart, took over the business and renamed it Beam & Hart Distillery. Among the bourbons they produced were Old Tub (rather prescient, considering how liquor was made during Prohibition), Pebbleford, Clear Springs, and D. M. Beam.

Around the turn of the century, the company was restructured and renamed Clear Spring Distillery, and it operated as such until it was closed by Prohibition. Jim Beam sold his interest in Clear Spring and purchased property at Clermont, where another victim of Prohibition, Echo Spring Distillery, had gone out of business. It was there that Beam and partners built a new facility after repeal. They called it the Jim Beam Distillery, and by 1934, Jim Beam bourbon was being made there.

When Jim Beam died in 1947, his son T. Jeremiah, who had been the company treasurer, assumed the presidency. He hired Booker Noe, his nephew and Jim Beam's grandson. Noe oversaw operations at the Churchill Distillery in Boston, Kentucky, which was purchased by Beam in 1953. Noe eventually became master distiller and developed the barrel-proof, small-batch Booker's bourbon. Today, Booker Noe's son, Fred, is master distiller at Jim Beam.

Jim Beam (both its Clermont and Boston locations) was sold in 1967 to American Tobacco. But Beam family members, including Baker and David Beam, who were distillers at the Clermont plant, continued to make whiskey for the company. Jim Beam is owned today by Beam Global, created out of parent company Fortune Brands.

Other Beams associated with other distilleries, including Parker and Craig Beam of Heaven Hill and Paul and Steve Beam of Limestone Branch, are members of the same distilling clan.

The Tour

With the opening of the American Stillhouse in September 2012, the Jim Beam tour changed completely. For years, no visitors were allowed in the working distillery. Happily, the tour has now gone to the other extreme, allowing hands-on interaction in the bourbon-making process.

The first stop is to buy tickets in the multistory Stillhouse, which features a replica column still that is actually a working elevator (imagine yourself evaporating and condensing as you ride). Visitors then board a bus for the short trip to the distillery. Along the way, your tour guide will narrate the impressive seven-generation distilling history of the Beam family. Fortunately, each visitor receives a card with pictures of the important players—from founder Jacob Beam to current master distiller Fred Noe—so you can keep track of who's who.

The bus arrives at a craft distillery within the larger distillery. Visitors are invited to scoop grain into a 750-gallon mash tub (the capacity of a regular mash tub at Beam is 10,000 gallons) and get a close-up of the small column still (producing about 3 gallons per minute) and the corresponding doubler. If production is at the right point, you might be able to help fill a barrel on the barrel porch behind the mini-distillery, or you might be asked to help dump a barrel. It's all pretty cool.

After covering the basics of the bourbon-making process in the mini-distillery, the tour moves on to the Big House, where Jim Beam is made. The 10,000-gallon-capacity mash tubs (or cookers) are making sour mash that will, in turn, be fermented into enough distiller's beer to keep the five-story-high column still turning out high wine at a rate of 200 gallons per minute. All this machinery is supervised by just two staff members seated in a computerized control room.

From the still house, the tour goes past the case house, a caged enclosure holding samples of all Beam products for a certain period of time—part of the distillery's quality-control regimen. Then you'll drop in on

Checking the color of Knob Creek during a tour tasting.

Bourbon being dumped from the barrel.

the action at one of the numerous bottling lines. There are so many lines bottling so many products that an HDTV monitor in the hallway keeps track of what's being bottled where. On a recent visit, bottling line J was packaging Jim Beam for shipment to Japan. Another monitor showed that 2,542 cases of product had been bottled by 10 a.m. on a shift that had started at 7:30.

Then it's back past the case house to an exhibit that no other distillery can match. You don't even have to be a bourbon drinker to enjoy the room lined with lighted shelves displaying row after row of the famous Beam decanters. Produced between 1953 and 1992, the porcelain and glass decanters were designed in the shapes of automobiles, each of the fifty states, animals, celebrities, and much more. And who knew that the bottle that actress Barbara Eden materialized from in the 1960s TV sit-com, *I Dream of Jeannie* was a Beam decanter? It has its own pedestal here.

After viewing the decanter exhibit, visitors are bused back to a state-of-the-art tasting room.

The Bourbon

Since Beam makes so many products and state law limits you to two samples, Beam has borrowed a tasting technology from the wine industry. Everyone is given a plastic card upon entering the tasting room, which is furnished with several machines that dispense a whiskey sample into your glass when you insert the card and push a button for

Bottles of Jim Beam wait in the bottling plant.

Bronze sculpture of the late Booker Noe, the master distiller who created Booker's bourbon.

the desired selection. Choices range from Jim Beam Black Label and Red Stag Spice to Devil's Cut and Booker's. Technically, Red Stag whiskies are not bourbons, since by law, "no additives of any kind can be used to flavor or color any bourbon." But that doesn't mean you won't enjoy them! Following are descriptions of some of the bourbons you can taste.

Baker's is aged for seven years and bottled at 107 proof, so adding a little water helps reveal its layers of dark fruit, vanilla, caramel, and more than a hint of chocolate. The dark amber Baker's has an appealing nuttiness, too.

Basil Hayden has a higher proportion of rye in its mash bill than the other Beam bourbons. The rye and the bottling of the eight-year-old bourbon at 80 proof combine to give it a light, spicy character. No water is needed to bring out its flavors.

Booker's is one *big* bourbon. Bottled at the proof at which it comes out of the barrel, it usually weighs in at between 121 and 127 proof. Aged six to eight years, it is characterized by powerful vanilla and oak, which evolve into rich toffee on the tongue. A splash of water helps reveal a hint of spice at the finish.

Devil's Cut is a play on "angels' share," since it is made with bourbon that would usually not escape from the barrel. After the bourbon is dumped, distilled water is added to the empty barrel, and a special process is used to extract the bourbon remaining in the red layer. The bourbon-flavored water is used to adjust the proof. The resulting 90-proof bourbon has rich vanilla, toasted pecan, and caramel notes.

Jim Beam Black Label is aged eight years—twice as long as the flagship White Label—and it is 90 proof. The adjective that works well for almost all aspects of its vanilla, corn, and oak notes is "toasty."

Knob Creek is aged nine years and is bottled at 100 proof. Plenty of fruits and nuts keep the vanilla and caramel company. A touch of water brings out the orange in the nose.

Travel Advice

If you are coming from Louisville, take I-65 south to exit 112 (KY 245). Turn left (east), and you'll see Jim Beam on your left in just under two miles. The trip takes about half an hour from downtown Louisville. Coming from Lexington, take the Bluegrass Parkway west to exit 25 (US 150) and drive toward Bardstown. Turn right onto KY 245 and drive thirteen and a half miles to the distillery, on your right. This takes about ninety minutes.

If you want to drive directly to Bardstown from Louisville, take

The office building of the now-closed Chapeze Distillery, which served as a movie set for Stripes *(1981).*

US 31E, which is Bardstown Road. It's a more scenic route and is actually a little faster than I-65.

Chapeze/Old Charter Distillery

About a mile's drive from Jim Beam, you can see what remains of the A. B. Chapeze Distillery, founded in 1867. The flagship bourbon brand was Old Charter, and the distillery was commonly referred to by that name. Like the vast majority of bourbon distilleries, it ceased production during Prohibition, although it did reopen after repeal and operated under various owners until 1951. The Old Charter brand produced today is made in Frankfort by Buffalo Trace.

Beam bought the property in 1970 and is still using the warehouses. A notable feature is the half-timbered-style building that once housed the distillery offices. The combination of the European-inflected architecture and the site's industrial feel made it a good location for filming the Russian outpost scene in the 1981 Bill Murray comedy *Stripes*. (Other Kentucky locations in the movie included Fort Knox and places around Louisville.) Who knew that a Kentucky bourbon distillery could stand in for Czechoslovakia?

To get to the former distillery, turn right as you leave Jim Beam, drive just over half a mile to the Forest Edge Winery, and turn right onto Chapeze Lane (County Road 3219). In another half mile you'll drive past the facility.

Bernheim Arboretum and Research Forest

Directly across the highway from the Jim Beam Distillery is a 14,000-acre forest subsidized by bourbon. German immigrant Isaac Wolfe Bernheim and his brother Bernard came to Kentucky in the nineteenth century and made a fortune from bourbon. The original Bernheim Distillery in Louisville produced I. W. Harper, Old Charter, Raven, and Mountain Dew (not to be confused with the fizzy green Pepsi product).

Bernheim felt tremendous gratitude to the city and state that allowed him to become a rich man. He and his brother were noted philanthropists, donating money to many local charitable causes. The statue of Thomas Jefferson that stands in front of the Jefferson County courthouse in downtown Louisville was one of their gifts. But their most lasting monument is a living one—**Bernheim Forest** (2499 KY 245, Clermont, 502-955-8512, www.bernheim.org).

Bernheim purchased the land, which had previously been farmed and logged, in 1928 and engaged the New York firm of Frederick Law

Fall color at Bernheim Forest.

Olmsted (designer of Louisville's parks system, as well as New York's Central Park) to design an arboretum. The landscaped portion of the facility is just a few minutes' drive from the entrance. The vast majority of the property is a natural, regrown hardwood forest crisscrossed by miles of hiking trails. It's a beautiful place for a break during your tour of bourbon country.

Acknowledgments

It would have been impossible for me to write and Pam Spaulding to photograph this book without the generous help of many, many people. From allowing us access to answering questions, everyone was unfailingly enthusiastic and obviously proud of Kentucky's bourbon culture. They are listed in alphabetical order by their institution:

Ken Pierce—Barton 1792; Dixon Dedman—Beaumont Inn; Joe Frase and Michael Grider—The Blind Pig; Matt Jamie—Bourbon Barrel Foods; Brian Gregory, Svend Jansen, Chris Morris, Mary Perkins, Greg Roshkowski, Kandi Sackett, and Marnie Walters—Brown-Forman and Woodford Reserve; Beau Beckman, Fred Mozenter, Amy Preske, Angela Traver, John Vereekee, and the Barrel Racing Team—Buffalo Trace; Kevin Hall—Distilled Spirits Epicenter; Michael Veach—Filson Historical Society; Brent Elliott, Patty Holland, Karen Kushner, Jim Rutledge, and Al Young—Four Roses; Lynne Grant, Larry Kass, Joe Skaggs, and Kathleen Smith—Heaven Hill; Lisa Marie Williams—Hill House Bed & Breakfast; Kimberley Bennett, Debbie Faust, Ginger Flowers, and Linda Hayes—Jim Beam; Drew Kulsveen—Kentucky Bourbon Distillers; Pam Glover, Linda Harrison, and Ann McMichael—Kentucky Bourbon Festival; Teri Smith and Jimmy Wickham—Kentucky Cooperage and Independent Stave; Eric Gregory—Kentucky Distillers' Association; Kathleen Neuhoff and Darkanyan and Shelley Wright—Kentucky Horse Park; Joyce Bender—Kentucky State Nature Preserves Commission; Barry McNees—Lexington Distillery District; Kathy Cary and Brad Jennings—Lilly's; Bryan Cushing, Carol Ely, and Gwynne Potts—Locust Grove; Jane Conner, Honi Goldman, and Bill Samuels Jr.—Maker's Mark; Lisa Frost and Joseph Magliocco—Michter's Distillery LLC; Charlotte Browning and Sean Higgins—Mint Julep Tours; Jennifer Broadwater, Aimee Darnell, and David Larson—Shaker Village of Pleasant Hill; Ben Jett and Cynthia Torp—Solid Light; Chris Lady, Ken Lee, Briana Stiff, and Tisha Surrett—Town Branch Distillery; Devona and Steve Porter—Tucker House Bed & Breakfast; Katrina Egbert, Jimmy Russell, Eddie Russell, and Alan Tenniswood—Wild Turkey.

Special thanks to Kathleen Neuhoff and Darkanyan, who allowed Pam to photograph them at the Kentucky Horse Park.

To those whose names didn't make it into my notebooks, please know that your help was greatly appreciated too!

Thanks, as well, to Laura Sutton, formerly of the University Press of Kentucky, for coming to me with the idea for this book and to her successor, Ashley Runyon, for guiding its production.

Finally, Joanna Goldstein helped in many, many ways, including as Pam's "voice-activated light stand," our traveling companion, and my bourbon-tasting partner.

Appendix A
More Resources for Bourbon Lovers

As bourbon has increased in popularity, so have the number of print and Internet publications devoted to bourbon. If you are interested in more history, news of releases, or tasting notes, or if you just want to share your love of bourbon with like-minded sippers, the following resources will help. These lists are by no means complete, but they will get you started with a good, basic bourbon library and help connect you to other bourbon fans.

Books

Campbell, Sally Van Winkle. *But Always Fine Bourbon: Pappy Van Winkle and the Story of Old Fitzgerald.* Louisville: Limestone Lane Press, 1999.

Bottle silhouette in shutters at Maker's Mark Distillery.

Carson, Gerald. *The Social History of Bourbon.* Foreword by Mike Veach. 1963. Reprint, Lexington: University Press of Kentucky, 2010.

Cecil, Sam K. *The Evolution of the Bourbon Whiskey Industry in Kentucky.* Paducah, KY: Turner Publishing, 1999.

Cowdery, Charles K. *Bourbon, Straight: The Uncut and Unfiltered Story of American Whiskey.* Chicago: Made & Bottled in Kentucky, 2004.

Crowgey, Henry G. *Kentucky Bourbon: The Early Years of Whiskeymaking.* 1971. Reprint, Lexington: University Press of Kentucky, 2008.

Givens, Ron. *Bourbon at Its Best: The Lore & Allure of America's Finest Spirits.* Cincinnati: Clerisy Press, 2008.

Nickell, Joe. *The Kentucky Mint Julep.* Lexington: University Press of Kentucky, 2003.

Perrine, Joy, and Susan Reigler. *The Kentucky Bourbon Cocktail Book.* Lexington: University Press of Kentucky, 2009.

Regan, Gary, and Mardee Haidin Regan. *The Book of Bourbon and Other Fine American Whiskies.* Shelburne, VT: Chapters Publishing, 1995.

Schmid, Albert W. A. *The Old Fashioned: An Essential Guide to the Original Whiskey Cocktail.* Lexington: University Press of Kentucky, 2012.

Veach, Michael R. *Kentucky Bourbon Whiskey: An American Heritage.* Lexington: University Press of Kentucky, 2013.

Zoeller, Chester. *Bourbon in Kentucky: A History and Directory of Distilleries in Kentucky.* Louisville: Butler Books, 2009.

View up a warehouse elevator shaft at Barton 1792.

Bourbon barrel art at Woodford Reserve.

Magazines

The Bourbon Country Reader. http://chuckcowdery.blogspot.com/.
The Bourbon Review. http://www.gobourbon.com.
F. Paul Pacult's Spirit Journal. http://www.spiritjournal.com.
Whisky Advocate. http://www.whiskyadvocate.com.
Whisky Magazine. http://www.whiskymag.com.

Websites and Blogs

Bourbon & Banter. http://bourbonbanter.com.
The Bourbon Babe. http://bourbonbabe.tumblr.com.
Bourbon Buzz. http://bourbonbuzz.com.
Bourbon Drinker. http://www.bourbondrinker.com.
Bourbon Enthusiast. http://www.bourbonenthusiast.com.
The Chuck Cowdery Blog. http://chuckcowdery.blogspot.com/.

A panel from Bourbon Women tasting samples for a private bottling at Four Roses.

The Sour Mash Manifesto. http://sourmashmanifesto.com.
Straight Bourbon. http://www.straightbourbon.com.
Whiskey.com. http://www.whisky.com/.
The Whiskey Professor. http://www.whiskeyprof.com.

Organizations

American Distilling Institute. 650-400-9812, http://www.distilling.com.
The Bourbon Society. http://www.thebourbonsociety.net.
Bourbon Women. 859-226-4255, http://www.bourbonwomen.org.
Kentucky Distillers' Association. 502-875-9351, http://www.kybourbon
    .com.

Appendix B
Bourbon Retailers

Although you can buy bottled bourbons in the gift shops of the distilleries, the selection is much greater at liquor stores. Of course, the average liquor store in Kentucky stocks a lot more bourbons than comparable retailers in other states. Some stores make a point of carrying a selection of limited-edition bottlings, and many have their own bottlings from personally selected barrels. The following liquor retailers are recommended for their quality and diversity. Most host frequent bourbon tastings, often with master distillers on hand, so contact them to see what they have on their calendars during your visit. Several also have information about their bourbon selections on their websites. Keep in mind that alcohol cannot be sold in Kentucky on Sundays until 1 p.m.

Louisville

Detail of a shutter at Barton 1792.

Liquor Barn
Springhurst, 4301 Towne Center Drive,
    502-426-4222
850 South Hurstbourne Parkway,
    502-491-0753
3420 Fern Valley Road, 502-968-1666
http://www.liquorbarn.com

Old Town Wine and Spirits
1529 Bardstown Road, 502-451-8591
http://www.oldtownwine.com

Party Mart
4808 Brownsboro Centre (US 42 and
    Watterson Expressway), 502-895-4446

Taste Fine Bourbons
634 East Market Street, 502-409-4644
http://tastefinewinesandbourbons.com

Taking a barrel "train ride" at the Kentucky Bourbon Festival.

Westport Whiskey & Wine
Westport Village, 1115 Herr Lane, 502-708-1313
http://www.westportwhiskeyandwine.com

The Wine Rack
2632 Frankfort Avenue, 502-721-9148
http://wineshoplouisville.com

Lexington

Liquor Barn
Hamburg Pavilion (at Man o' War Boulevard), 1837 Plaudit Place,
    859-294-5700
Harrodsburg Road at New Circle, 921 Beaumont Centre Parkway,
    859-223-1400

3040 Richmond Road, 859-269-4170
http://www.liquorbarn.com

Shoppers Village Liquors
1601 North Broadway, 859-293-0344

The Thoroughbred Shop
2005 Versailles Road, 859-254-0358

Frankfort

Capital Cellars
227 West Broadway, 502-352-2600
http://capitalcellars.net/

Red Dot Wine & Spirits
Century Plaza, 1139 US 127, 502-227-4001
740 Schenkel Lane, 502-223-5054
http://www.reddotky.com

Bardstown

Keystone Liquors
130 Keystone Avenue,
502-348-3164

Liquor World
93 North Salem Drive,
502-349-7560

Barrels from the Bourbon Festival's sponsors.

Kathleen Neuhoff rides Darkanyan,
grandson of Seattle Slew, at the
Kentucky Horse Park.

Glossary

The Bourbon Lexicon

angels' share: The liquid that evaporates from aging barrels (the proportion of whiskey and water depends on the barrel's location in the warehouse). Typically, about 10 percent of the total evaporates the first year, and 3 to 4 percent each year thereafter.

backset: A watery portion of a previously distilled mash that has been saved and is added ("set back") to a new batch of fermenting mash (similar to a sourdough starter).

barrel proof: Bourbon that is bottled directly from the barrel without adding water to adjust the proof. Because of evaporation during aging, the proof is typically high.

beading: The formation of bubbles when a bottle of bourbon is shaken. The larger the bubbles that form at the top, the higher the proof.

beer: See **distiller's beer.**

beer still: A still used to produce low wines from distiller's beer. If it is a column still, it will be several stories high. If it is one of a series of pot stills, it will be the largest. The distillate is typically about 40 proof.

bonded bourbon (also **bottled in bond**): Originally, bourbon that was produced in a government-bonded warehouse for taxing purposes. Now it refers to a bourbon that is at least four years old and at least 100 proof. In addition, it must be the product of one distillery and one distiller in one season.

bottled in bond: See **bonded bourbon.**

bourbon: American whiskey made from a fermented grain mash that is at least 51 percent corn. Its final distillation can be no higher than

160 proof, and it must be put in new (unused) charred oak barrels at no higher than 125 proof. There is no age requirement. As soon as the whiskey touches wood, it becomes bourbon. Note that almost no bourbon made today is aged for less than four years. See also **straight bourbon**.

bung: The stopper used to seal a barrel. It is made of yellow poplar because it expands when soaked with liquid.

charring: The process in which the interior of a barrel is set on fire and allowed to burn for less than a minute. This cracks and blackens the wood, which allows the whiskey to penetrate the sides of the barrel.

chill haze: The cloudiness that appears at cool temperatures (such as when ice is added) if a bourbon is unfiltered or only lightly filtered.

congeners: The esters and fusel oils, mostly by-products of fermentation, that add flavor to bourbons. Tiny amounts are optimal; too much can produce off flavors.

continuous still: Another term for the **beer still**.

cooper: A barrel maker.

cooperage: Facility where barrels are made.

corn whiskey: Whiskey made from 80 to 100 percent corn mash and aged in used or uncharred barrels.

distillation: Production of alcohol through a series of steps involving evaporation and condensation.

distiller's beer: Liquid from the fermented mash that is ready to be distilled to make whiskey. The alcohol content is usually between 8 and 10 percent, or 16 to 20 proof.

dona tub: A container in which yeast is grown until it reaches sufficient volume to be added to the mash.

doubler: The copper still to which low wines from the beer still are added to produce high wines (i.e., new whiskey).

doublings: Another term for **high wines**.

esters: Aromatic organic compounds produced by yeast as a by-product of fermentation. They are responsible for many of the fruity and spicy flavors in whiskey.

expressions: Different versions of a whiskey brand that vary by age or proof. For example, Old Forester comes in 86- and 100-proof expressions.

fermenter: The large tank, typically made of stainless steel or cypress wood, in which cooked mash is fermented by yeast.

fusel oils: These alcohols, with a higher molecular weight than beverage alcohol, are present in tiny amounts in whiskey distillate. Higher amounts can produce off flavors.

heads and tails: The first and last distillates to come off the doubler, respectively. Since both contain impurities, they are returned to the still for further distillation. In some premium bourbons, the heads and tails are discarded rather than being distilled again.

Four Roses bottling line at Cox's Creek.

high wines: The spirits, also called new whiskey, produced in the doubler; they can be put into barrels for aging. High wines cannot be more than 160 proof.

low wines: The spirits produced by the first distillation of **distiller's beer.**

malted barley (or simply **malt**): Partially sprouted barley that is roasted to stop germination. It is added to the mash bill to facilitate fermentation, since barley contains enzymes not found in corn, rye, or wheat. These enzymes help the yeast convert starch to fermentable sugars and then to alcohol.

mash: The mixture of grains cooked in the mash tub until it resembles porridge.

mash bill: The recipe, or the proportion of each grain used to produce a particular whiskey.

mash tub: The large metal (usually stainless steel) vessel in which the grains are cooked.

master distiller: The bourbon maker assigned the overall responsibility for production and quality at a particular distillery.

mingling: The process of mixing bourbon from several barrels to create a consistent flavor profile. This is different from "blending," which is the process of adding flavors or aged spirits to grain-neutral spirits. By law, bourbons are never blended.

new whiskey: The clear distillate from the final distillation that is put into barrels for aging. Also called **high wine** or **doublings**.

nose: The combination of aromas that can be detected by smelling bourbon in a glass. Equivalent to a wine's bouquet.

Prohibition: The period in American history when the sale of beverage alcohol was illegal. The Volstead Act was passed in 1919 to enforce the Eighteenth Amendment to the Constitution, which made Prohibition federal law. Prohibition was repealed on December 5, 1933, with ratification of the Twenty-First Amendment.

Top of the column still at Four Roses Distillery in Lawrenceburg.

proof: Measure of the percentage of alcohol in a beverage, based on a 200-point scale. Thus, 90-proof bourbon is 45 percent alcohol by volume. The term (and the numbers) originated in the nineteenth century when buyers, seeking to verify that their whiskey had not been diluted, would mix it with gunpowder and light it. It would burn only if the whiskey was at least 50 percent alcohol, thus providing 100 percent "proof" that it was undiluted.

rackhouse (also **rickhouse**): A warehouse where bourbon is stored for aging.

rectified whiskey: Spirits mixed and sold by a rectifier.

rectifier: Historically, a spirits dealer who purchased whiskies from one or more distillers and mixed them to make the desired product. This practice was common in the nineteenth century, when most distilleries were small and could make a profit only by selling to rectifiers.

red layer: The layer of caramelized wood sugars formed when a barrel is charred. This gives bourbon its color and much of its flavor.

repeal: The end of Prohibition, which took effect on December 5, 1933, when Utah became the thirty-fifth state to ratify the Twenty-First Amendment to the Constitution. Repeal was made possible by the Blaine Act, introduced to Congress by Senator John Blaine of Wisconsin.

ricks: The scaffolding made of wooden beams on which aging barrels rest in a warehouse.

rye whiskey: Whiskey made from a mash bill containing at least 51 percent rye.

setback: See **backset**.

single barrel: Whiskey bottled from a single barrel. The yield can range from 60 to 150 750-mL bottles, depending on how long the whiskey was aged and how much was lost to evaporation.

small batch: Whiskey bottled from the mingling of a small number of barrels. There is no prescribed number: some distilleries make small batches from as few as ten barrels, and others may use a hundred or more.

small grains (or **smalls**): The grains other than corn, usually malted barley and rye or wheat, used to make bourbon and Tennessee whiskey.

sour mash: See **backset**.

spent mash: The grain residue left over after fermentation; also known as spent beer or stillage. Because spent mash is rich in carbohydrates and proteins, many distilleries sell it or give it away to local farmers, who use it for animal feed.

spirit safe: A glass-walled brass box that allows distillers access to distilling spirits to measure the density. Otherwise, the safe is kept locked.

straight bourbon: Bourbon that has been aged at least two years before bottling.

sweet mash: Mash fermented without the addition of backset.

tails: See **heads and tails.**

Tennessee whiskey: Whiskey that is almost identical to bourbon, with the same mash bill and aging requirements, but before it is put in the barrel, it is filtered through sugar maple charcoal. The two remaining distilleries that produce Tennessee whiskey are located in (surprise!) Tennessee: Jack Daniels (in Lynchburg) and George Dickel (in Cascade Hollow near Tullahoma).

thief: A copper tube that can be inserted into a barrel of aging whiskey to extract a sample for evaluation.

thumper: A second still to which uncondensed low-wine vapors from the beer still are added and bubbled through hot water before being condensed and distilled into high wines. It has the same function as a **doubler**.

toasting: Process of heating oak staves so they can be bent to make barrels.

Volstead Act: See **Prohibition**.

warehouse staining: Dark coloring on the walls of warehouses and other structures near a distillery that results from the growth of a

Culture of Old Forester's proprietary yeast strain in the Early Times Distillery lab.

harmless microscopic fungus, *Baudoinia compniacensis,* that feeds on evaporated alcohol.

wheated bourbon: Bourbon in which wheat has been substituted for rye in the mash bill.

yeast: Microscopic, single-celled fungi (*Saccharomyces cerevisiae*) that feed on the sugars present in mash. The by-products of their digestion are ethyl alcohol, carbon dioxide, heat, and a variety of fruity-smelling compounds (esters), depending on the yeast strain. Some distilleries, such as Brown-Forman, propagate their yeast on-site from frozen or liquid cultures. Others, including Buffalo Trace, add cakes of dry yeast directly to their fermenters.

Index